The Great Ridley Rescue

the great
RIDLEY RESCUE

by Pamela Phillips • illustrated by Janie Lowe

MOUNTAIN PRESS PUBLISHING COMPANY

1989

Library of Congress Cataloging-in-Publication Data

Phillips, Pamela.
    The great ridley rescue.

    Bibliography: p.
    Includes index.

    Summary: Describes the history and habitat of the Kemp's ridley turtle and past and present
efforts of humans to save it from extinction.

    1. Lepidochelys kempii—Juvenile literature. 2. Wildlife rescue—Juvenile literature.
3. Sea turtles—Juvenile literature, [1, Atlantic ridley turtle. 2. Sea turtles. 3. Turtles.
4. Rare animals. 5 Wildlife conservation] I. Lowe, Janie, ill. II. Title

QL666.C536P45   1988   639.9'7792   88-13635
ISBN 0-87842-229-3 (pbk.)

MOUNTAIN PRESS PUBLISHING COMPANY
P.O. Box 2399
Missoula, Montana 59806

Dedications

Of the Author. . .

For Leon, who took me to Galveston to see Kemp's ridleys and buy sea turtle T-shirts for our sons in New Zealand, and for Janie's mother Katherine, who sat next to me at a literary luncheon in Lubbock and said she thought her daughter in Colorado would love to illustrate a book on sea turtles.

Of the Illustrator. . .

For the loved ones I lived with and without while I worked on this book: Mom, Dad and Tom.

Contents

List of Boxes

Foreword

In the last ten years, 13,722 healthy yearling Kemp's ridleys, *Lepidochelys kempi*, from the Sea Turtle Head Start Research Project have been released into the Gulf of Mexico, thanks to international cooperation among the Mexican government, three United States federal agencies and a state agency, biologists, conservationists and volunteers. Head starting protects the turtles through their first high-risk year of life, thus they avoid exposure to the many natural predators that they would otherwise be confronted with in the wild during this time. The project is part of an international effort to save Kemp's ridley from extinction.

Head starting is an experiment through which we hope to establish a new nesting colony on Padre Island, Texas, to supplement the only known nesting aggregation at Rancho Nuevo, Tamaulipas, on Mexico's Gulf of Mexico coast. In addition, several hundred head started Kemp's ridleys have been translocated to the Cayman Turtle Farm and to other marine aquaria to build a captive brood stock as a safety net for the species. The now 9-year-old ridleys at the farm on Grand Cayman Island, British West Indies, have produced hundreds of hatchlings, some of which have been head started at the National Marine Fisheries Service's Laboratory in Galveston, Texas.

In her account of the Kemp's ridley story, the author describes the history and natural history of Kemp's ridley, the Mexican and United States conservation efforts at Rancho Nuevo, the various stages of "Operation Head Start," the main hazards facing the turtles in the past and at present, and the ways in which readers can help prevent extinction of this critically endangered species. She has striven to make it technically accurate while retaining easy readability. This book is an important addition to the popular literature on sea turtles.

Charles W. Caillouet, Jr., Ph.D.
Chief, Life Studies Division
National Marine Fisheries Service
Galveston Laboratory
Galveston, Texas, July 1988

I A Head Start For Survival

A HOT, HAZY MORNING on the Gulf of Mexico, the air smelling of salt, sea-life and diesel exhaust. A small, cream-and-black sea turtle falls into the green waters of the Gulf with an ungraceful splash, rights itself after a moment of confusion, then dives and swims away from the chugging boat. The marine biologist who launched it wipes a droplet of sweat from the tip of his nose and reaches for another turtle, while a television cameraman solemnly records the event for the five o'clock news. A lone seagull that has swooped to investigate gives a disappointed cry and flies off towards the distant line of scrubby dunes that is Padre Island.

The little turtle swims away strongly, even though this particular survivor from the age of the dinosaurs has been away from the ocean for over ten months. It was recaptured with a hand-net during its first brief 'imprinting' swim as a hatchling, and until now has led an uncommonly sheltered life. The egg it hatched from was placed under armed, military protection at the moment of laying, made the subject of high-level government deliberations and incredibly elaborate documentation, ferried from Mexico to Texas by private airplane, and incubated under controlled laboratory conditions at Padre Island. The new hatchling's first twenty-second swim was preceded by a well-guarded scramble down a Padre Island beach and followed by a tedious car journey to Galveston, where it has lived until now in a bright yellow bucket and been treated much more carefully than a hotel guest.

It has been weighed and measured regularly, fed on steadily increasing amounts of nourishing turtle chow, and nursed back to health when it became sick. And at last, practically bristling with identification tags, it has been driven back to Padre Island and loaded onto a boat with several hundred of its contemporaries for an undignified but effective return to the sea. In future years, if it is found sick or injured on a beach around the Gulf, it will be rehabilitated by experts. If it remains too long in the colder waters off the north-eastern coast of the United States, so

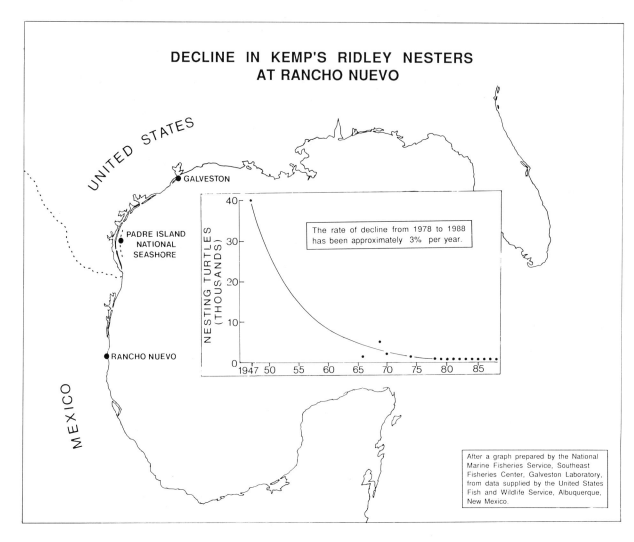

DECLINE IN KEMP'S RIDLEY NESTERS AT RANCHO NUEVO

UNITED STATES

GALVESTON

PADRE ISLAND
NATIONAL
SEASHORE

RANCHO NUEVO

MEXICO

The rate of decline from 1978 to 1988 has been approximately 3% per year.

NESTING TURTLES (THOUSANDS)

40
30
20
10
0
1947 50 55 60 65 70 75 80 85

After a graph prepared by the National Marine Fisheries Service, Southeast Fisheries Center, Galveston Laboratory, from data supplied by the United States Fish and Wildlife Service, Albuquerque, New Mexico.

Graph showing decline in Kemp's ridley nesters at Rancho Nuevo.

that it becomes incapable of swimming and is cast up on a beach, it will stand a good chance of being found by a beach walker or volunteer patrol, revived, and flown home. And if it is unfortunate enough to be caught and drowned in a fishing net, the tags will ensure that its fate is known.

Nearly two thousand Kemp's ridley sea turtles receive this special treatment each year and have done so since 1978, as part of a remarkable effort to save the species from extinction. This is because, whereas six of the eight species of sea turtle in the world are regarded as endangered, Kemp's ridley is the most seriously threatened of all. In 1947, when its nesting was first filmed on a remote beach near Rancho Nuevo in Mexico, up to 40,000 turtles nested in one day. The impact of humans on both eggs and turtles caused this number to dwindle to 1,500 by 1966, and a further drop to about 250 turtles nesting in a day had occurred by 1977. In 1978, Mexico and the United States joined forces to devise conservation measures. Even after ten years of joint action, the number of nesting females continues to decrease at a rate of about three percent per year. In 1987, fewer than 600 turtles nested along the 20-mile stretch of beach during the entire three-month nesting season.

Operation Head Start is a part of the international conservation plan. This project is an attempt to establish a second nesting colony at Padre Island National Seashore, near Corpus Christi in Texas, by incubating Rancho Nuevo eggs in Padre Island sand and imprinting their hatchlings in Padre Island sand and sea water. For this project Mexico makes a gift of 2,000 Rancho Nuevo eggs to the United States government each year. The eggs are flown to Padre Island for incubation and imprinting, and the hatchlings are reared in captivity in Galveston for their most vulnerable first ten months, before being released at sea off Padre Island.

It is hoped that the imprinted turtles will ultimately return to nest at Padre Island, obeying the same kind of instinct that allows salmon to locate the river in which they themselves hatched when it is time to return to fresh water for spawning. The presence of a second colony nesting at Padre Island would greatly improve the chances of survival of the species in the event of the primary nesting beach at Rancho Nuevo suffering a major disaster such as an oil spill, a hurricane, flooding or erosion.

IMPRINTING

"Imprinting" is the name given to a part of the process that produces a homing instinct in species as diverse as pigeons and salmon. Very little is known about how it works, or how it affects sea turtles. Biologists speculate that the little turtles, either in the egg or as hatchlings, may use their keen senses to learn enough about the characteristic smell, taste, feel, or other properties of the sand or sea at their nesting beach to enable them to return there. Later, when it is their time to nest, they instinctively sense where they are at sea and use some unknown means of navigation to find their way home to the nesting beach. Experiments with pigeons suggest that several different kinds of directional cue may be involved at the same time, including phenomena as esoteric as the phase difference between circadian and diurnal rhythms, polarization of sunlight reflected from clouds, and the direction of the earth's magnetic field.

As far as Kemp's ridley turtles are concerned, laboratory tests, by a team led by Professor David Owens of the Texas A&M University's Department of Biology at College Station, have shown that four-month-old Padre Island-imprinted turtles, given the choice, prefer to be in sandy seawater from Padre Island rather than in similar water from some other place.

Owens comments: "These experiments support the theory, but I have not done any work with adults, so it could be said that the whole idea of imprinting in sea turtles remains hypothetical at present.

"Because Rancho Nuevo is the only major nesting site, some biologists interpret this as evidence for imprinting. Others contend that the nesting turtles find the beach by following experienced adults. Both factors could be involved.

"A female rarely changes her nesting beach, but can learn to nest elsewhere. This shows that if imprinting occurs it is not irreversible. Both head started Kemp's ridleys and wild adult green turtles taken to the Cayman Island turtle farm have nested there."

II The Riddle Of The Ridley

AN AIR OF MYSTERY surrounded the Kemp's ridley sea turtle for much of this century. Its nesting place remained a secret, there were no reports of turtles containing eggs when they were caught by fishermen, and very few people had seen hatchlings. Biologists knew that some young Kemp's ridleys drifted with the Florida Current into the Gulf Stream and up the coast as far as Newfoundland, and some even stayed with the current for a 3000-mile journey to Europe, but nobody knew where the journey began.

The origin of the name 'ridley' or 'ridler', used by fishermen, remains undetermined. Professor Archie Carr speculated that ridler might have been an earlier stage in the evolution of the name. Ridley could be a corruption of riddler, something that presents a riddle. The turtle was called Kemp's ridley after Richard Kemp of Key West, who sent the type specimen[1] to Samuel Garman at Harvard in 1880. Its most common name was probably the 'bastard turtle', because fishermen thought it was a hybrid between a loggerhead and a hawksbill or green turtle. This kind of turtle would struggle to the point of death when captured and laid on its back on deck, and fishermen believed that it died of a broken heart; thus it came to be known as the heart-break turtle.

Kemp's ridleys often were caught with green turtles in nets strung across channels along the coast of the Gulf of Mexico from Texas to Florida, and by trawlers along the coasts of the Gulf of Mexico and southeastern states on the Atlantic. The green turtle, which made excellent soup, was canned as soup and meat in south Texas in the second half of the last century. The ridley was eaten locally.

The Hunt for a Nesting Ground

Two leading American turtle biologists, Archie Carr and Henry Hildebrand, led the hunt for the Kemp's ridley nesting ground. The late Professor Carr, from the University of Florida, first became interested in the Kemp's ridley in 1938, after a friend at a shark-processing factory had complained about an aggressively snapping sea-turtle that some fisher-men brought in for shark bait. In appearance Carr was very close to the image of everybody's favorite professor. He was slim (one of his friends goes further and describes him as extraordinarily lean), distinguished-looking and scholarly, of about average height, with glasses and sparse grey hair. We are told that photographs do not do justice to his mobile face, very blue eyes and keen sense of humor, and that his enjoyment of life was intense and infectious. His personality was very friendly and outgoing, so that he could fit into almost any group; his presence and his reputation in the field were such that, when he spoke, everybody listened. His enthusuiasm too was infectious. Jack Rudloe[2], writing of an early conversation with Carr, says: "Before I knew it, I had agreed to tag ridleys and other sea turtles that came my way."

Carr talked to zoologists, to fishermen from Boston to the Mississippi and all over the Caribbean, and to men who slaughtered turtles for the market. None had ever seen a ridley nesting, or found a female containing eggs. He described this "riddle of the ridley" in his book *The Windward Road* in 1956, when he was nearing the end of a twenty-year search for ridley flipper tracks on beaches on both sides of the Atlantic, in the Gulf of Mexico and in the Caribbean. He discounted the fishermen's theory that the ridley was not a separate species but merely a hybrid of two other turtles. But, as he wrote plaintively in a report of that period:

"It once seemed to me that the mystery would have to wait until somebody stumbled on masses of ridleys ganged up in an overlooked place, perversely carrying out their sex rites in secret."

Professor Henry Hildebrand, from the now-closed University of Corpus Christi, had read *The Windward Road* with great interest, and for some years had been conducting a separate search for ridley nests along the south Texan and Mexican Gulf coasts. He had heard from the Marine Biology Station in the state of Veracruz about isolated ridley nestings there.

Hildebrand is also of medium height and an academic, but there the resemblance to Carr ends. Solidly built, with fair hair, he is a rather quiet, self-effacing person, with a friendly, full–cheeked face and eyes accustomed to squinting into the Texas sun. Fluent in Spanish (with a strong Texan accent), he was instantly accepted in Mexico, where he interacted with the rural people in a notably friendly and unpretentious way. Hildebrand, who had a strong explorer streak, was to unravel the Kemp's ridley mystery with dogged persistence over many years. He continues to be a leading naturalist with a great concern for marine life.

Virgil Mercer, a friend of Hildebrand's, had flown over the beaches of Veracruz many times. He told Hildebrand that around his camp at

Professor Carr, holding a turtle

Cabo Rojo, in the northern part of the state, flipper tracks from various species of turtle were especially numerous, and egg gathering there was so intense that Mercer expected the turtles to become extinct. As a result, Hildebrand's interest now focussed on the most inaccessible and least developed beaches on the Gulf of Mexico, which stretched southwards for about 255 miles from Matamoros, on the United States border, to Tampico in the state of Tamaulipas. No significant ports or villages existed on this coastline and commercial fishing was at a minimum. Cattle ranches did extend to the beaches but the ranch buildings were located inland to escape hurricane damage.

From Vincent Stevenson, who had operated a fishing camp in the north of the area since 1935, Hildebrand learned that the turtles nesting in the northernmost 155 miles were not ridleys. During a fisheries survey in 1958, Hildebrand went farther south, staying with Francis McDonald, who had run the Campo Andrés fishing camp at Barra del Tordo since 1948.

McDonald told him that such large numbers of small tortugas nested at the same time near his camp that an Arab trader came each year with about fifty burros to pack out gunny sacks full of eggs, which he sold

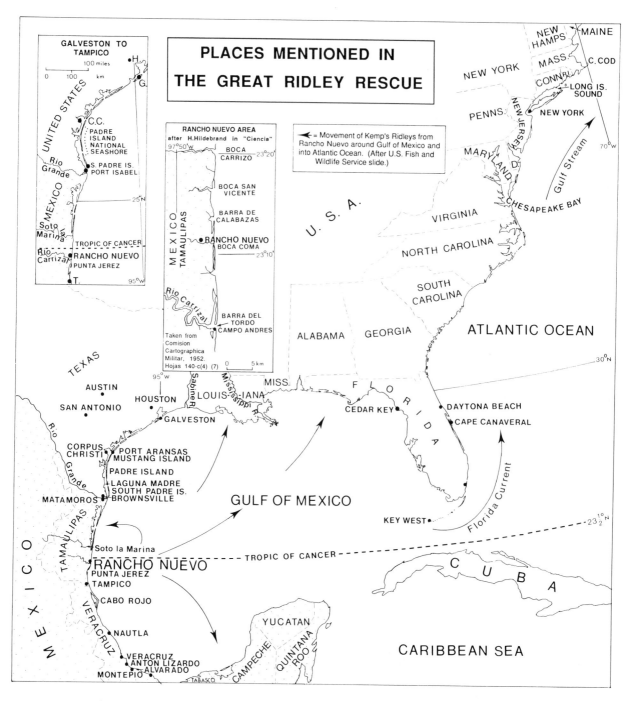

Map of Gulf of Mexico and the Atlantic Coast of the United States. Insets: enlargements of the Tamaulipas-Texas coastline and of the Rancho Nuevo area.

in Tampico. An odd feature of the story was that the turtles nested in broad daylight, which no species was then known to do.

One of McDonald's fishing guides, who had eight years' experience at the camp, said that turtles nested by the hundreds near the camp and by the thousands near Rancho Nuevo, farther north. McDonald himself estimated that the number of turtles nesting locally was in the thousands. The small size of the nesting turtles indicated to Hildebrand that they almost certainly were ridleys. Evidently the names tortuga (= turtle) and cahauma were used by the local people for the Kemp's ridley. Complete verification came in the fall of 1960, when Hildebrand was given the carapace of a ridley that had nested at Campo Andrés, and Mrs Oscar Eldridge, of Beaumont, Texas, lent him a movie film she had made of one of the ridleys she had seen nesting there.

Professor Carr also found some encouraging leads in the late fifties. At last a Florida fisherman reported an adult female ridley carrying eggs, and two University of Kansas students reported that a pair of baby ridleys had been caught by fishermen near Veracruz, on the south-west Mexican Gulf coast. The Carr family went to the Veracruz area to investigate, looking along the beaches for tracks and searching garbage dumps for shells and bones. They found three red-painted ridley shells nailed to a wall in a shop and were told they had belonged to turtles that were caught on the beach when they came to lay eggs. Mexicans told them that this cotorra or lora nested singly at Nautla, Anton Lizardo, Alvarado and Montepio in the state of Veracruz. In this part of the country, they found, tortuga was the name used for the green turtle.[3]

Bypassing the northern Mexican Gulf coast, Carr now began to hunt on Padre Island, Texas, talking to a fisherman who had seen turtle tracks as he drove along the beach. In a gift shop in Port Isabel he came upon five large ridley shells that Mexican shrimpers had sold to the owner. To his surprise, shrimpers at the docks who examined them said they belonged to the lora or cotorra, the only kind of turtle common thereabouts. They were frequently caught in shrimp trawls close to the shore in spring and early summer, and the females often had eggs inside them when they were butchered.

On Carr's return to Florida, his colleague Larry Ogren showed him a paper that had been overlooked by the biologists hunting for the nesting ground. The paper reported the nesting of a ridley at Padre Island on June 3rd, 1948, as observed by Jesse Laurence, the County Engineer at Corpus Christi, and it had been published in 1951 by John Werler[4] of the San Antonio Zoological Society.

Laurence had found a turtle laying a hundred eggs, fifty yards above the high tide line, while he was driving a jeep along the beach at Big Shell to collect engineering data. Eighteen of the eggs had been dug up and incubated in a bucket of sand and two little turtles had hatched after fifty-eight days. Carr then telephoned Laurence, who said he had discovered a second nesting turtle nearby at Little Shell on May 23, 1950. On that occasion, twenty-seven of the hundred eggs had been put in a basket of sand, and five had hatched after sixty-two days. Laurence sent Carr a photograph which confirmed that the turtles were ridleys.

Hildebrand had heard independently of one Kemp's ridley nesting at Corpus Christi Pass and two between Big and Little Shell on Padre Island, where beach conditions were so difficult that cars could rarely get through. Like Carr, he had heard stories which led him to believe that a large turtle rookery might have existed in the past at Montepio. There were vague hints, but no solid evidence, of a second one at Padre Island.

Meanwhile, the Campo Andrés stories had led Hildebrand to Señor Andrés Herrera, from Tampico. Andrés Herrera's family have owned ranches in the state of Veracruz for generations; he has also run a road construction company for many years, and has been flying since he was very young. Herrera had landed his plane on the beach near Rancho Nuevo, about 200 miles south of the border, in June, 1947, to take a movie film of an enormous crowd of nesting turtles. For Hildebrand, Herrera's film was a bombshell. At Hildebrand's invitation, Carr flew from Florida to see the film and confirmed that the turtles were Kemp's ridleys.

"You could have run a whole mile down the beach on the backs of turtles and never have set foot on the sand," wrote Carr, describing the film in his book *So Excellent a Fishe*. "And because sand was flying, and because ridleys are frisky, petulant nesters.... the scene was charged with feverish activity. The ridleys seemed more like over-wrought creatures searching for something lost than like turtles about the business of pro-creation."

Soon afterwards, in 1961, Hildebrand showed the film at a meeting of the American Society of Ichthyologists and Herpetologists[5] in Austin, Texas. He told members of the society that marine biologists were forever indebted to Señor Herrera for recording the spectacular natural history sight before the numbers of Kemp's ridleys were greatly depleted by man.

"Urgent conservation measures are needed to save even the vast arribadas[6] of the ridley from extinction," wrote Hildebrand in 1963, when he published his discovery and gave the first description of the nesting ground in the Mexican journal *Ciencia* (as a contribution from the Technological Institute of Veracruz). It would not be long before the world would learn that Kemp's ridley had become the heart-break turtle for another reason: intentional and accidental destruction by man was driving it to the brink of extinction.

Andrés Herrera flies over a large arribada on Rancho Nuevo beach in 1947.

III The Arribada Of 1947

On JUNE 18, 1947, for the thirty-third time in two years, Señor Andrés Herrera flew his small plane along the 90-mile stretch of beach near Rancho Nuevo, determined to photograph a large arribada[6] of turtles. He had heard from local people that arribadas appeared at different points along the beach between late April and late June. Nearly two months earlier he had waited on the beach, in the hope of filming the first arribada of the year, but it appeared on April 26 a few hours after he returned to Tampico. Since then he had flown thirty consecutive days without seeing another.

"Sometimes I landed and some other I flew over the beach trying to spot the turtles in the sea," he recalls. "I remember watching the turtles from the air while flying over the area. During four or five days before the arribada they began to concentrate right in front of the precise spot where they laid their eggs. They looked like confetti floating on the surface of the sea."

The local people, who did not share his bird's eye view, watched for the appearance of *Sargassum* weed on the beach. The high winds that usually prevailed at the time of an arribada caused the floating weed to drift onto the beach, and the people took this as a sign that an arribada might be imminent.

On June 18 a remarkable sight appeared beneath the plane. About a mile from Barra de Calabazas (Pumpkin Creek), a few miles north of Rancho Nuevo, turtles were massed on the wind-swept beach for more than a mile. When Herrera landed he found Mexicans gathering piles of eggs and occasionally riding two or three feet on the backs of the creatures as they lumbered to and from their nests. The turtles were so densely packed that they crawled over each other, kicked sand into their neighbors' faces as they excavated and covered nesting holes, and dug up one another's eggs.

The turtles were on the beach from 9 a.m. to about 1 p.m., Herrera told Hildebrand later. They laid their eggs in a mile-long stretch of sand dune about 60ft wide, which rose from the low-lying beach to a height of about 3ft on its seaward side and 5ft on the landward side. Along this strip there were so many eggs in the subsurface sand that they could be found by digging anywhere. When Herrera returned to his plane after he had finished filming, he could not take off immediately because turtles were crawling around and under it.

"I landed between 10 a.m. and 1 p.m. with my friend Francisco Ruiz Garza and I was delayed one hour. It could have been much longer but after one hour I decided to push my plane along the shore to the point where I was finally free of turtles in order to be able to take off. Because there was no more room for the hundreds of turtles coming out of the sea, some of them crossed the sand dune where they died, drowned in a marsh."

As in most years, there was also a third arribada.

"I am not sure on the exact date of the third arribada but I do remember that I was ready to fly again when the man that was in charge of the 25-hour check of my plane had already uncovered the engine before he knew I had plans to leave. I was able to fly the day after, just to find out I had missed the third arribada by a day.

"I knew I was trying to record something out of the ordinary and I remember having conversations about the arribada and showing the film (I knew it was worth seeing) whenever I felt it would be of interest to somebody. I knew I had a story to tell but I sure did not imagine (how could I?) I had recorded an event of tremendous importance for the marine researchers. In that sense I kept the film in my drawer... "

Fourteen years later, after Hildebrand saw the film and talked to Herrera, he estimated that a total of forty thousand turtles had nested on the beach between 9 a.m. and 1 p.m. that day, with up to ten thousand turtles on shore at the same time.

The scene at hatching time should also have been quite spectacular. Allowing a hundred eggs to a nest, and assuming that fifty percent had hatched and that ten percent of the hatchlings succumbed to predators on the beach, the number of turtle hatchlings entering the sea over the space of a few days, about two months after this arribada, would have been close to two million.

Hildebrand at Rancho Nuevo

Hildebrand rode into Rancho Nuevo on horseback on June 26, 1961, after flying to Campo Andrés in one of Herrera's planes. Rancho Nuevo

Professor Hildebrand on horseback at Rancho Nuevo beside ridley tracks.

was a small village of about a hundred people, two miles from the beach and fifty miles north of Tampico. Six days earlier he had seen eight nesting turtles as he flew into the camp for a day, and had watched ninety-four hatchlings emerge from a transplanted nest. Both McDonald and Herrera had advised him to return for the full moon on June 28, in the hope that he would see the last arribada of the season, but the arribada had come on June 25, the day before he arrived.

Local ranchers said that arribadas occurred within a few days of a full moon, at a time when a strong wind was blowing from the northeast. They believed that the turtles knew that the high tides associated with a full moon would give them less distance to crawl and that the wind and tide would be likely to cover their tracks before they could be found by coyotes. Herrera says they could be correct, but the arribadas he verified took place a day before or after the last phase of the moon in April and June. Hildebrand surmised that daytime nesting might have developed as a defense against the nocturnal coyote.

He and Juan Gonzales Galvan, his host at Rancho Nuevo, rode along the 20-mile nesting beach during the next few days, watching for the single and small-group nestings that occurred between arribadas. Gonzales had watched arribadas for 25 years and learned about earlier ones from the older settlers. In his opinion, the heavier surf on windy days helped the turtles to come out of the water onto the beach.

Together they counted 84 faint tracks from the arribada, but found only one nest because men or coyotes had taken the others. As they watched a single hatchling from an earlier nesting make its way to the sea, Gonzales told Hildebrand that the hatchlings' main enemies, beside the coyote, were the black vulture, the ghost crab and the schools of fish that waited beyond the breakers at hatching time. Packs of coyotes patrolled the beaches watching for arribadas, and returned again at hatching time.

Hildebrand studied the nesting grounds intently, making notes for his paper that would appear in the Mexican journal in 1963. Because of the beach's isolation, the short time that arribadas were on shore, and the winds that covered over the light trails in the hard-packed sand, more than three quarters of a century would have passed between the published descriptions of the species and of its principal nesting ground.

Mexican caring for several sacks of eggs on Rancho Nuevo beach.

"So we didn't see an arribada, and I haven't seen one since, even though I have visited the beach several times during the past twenty years, " he told the author. "They don't occur on any precise date and one might have to remain at Rancho Nuevo for a month to see one. Gonzales told me that there were three large arribadas every nesting season. For each one the turtles dug up a different portion of the shore to lay their eggs."

Hildebrand's concern mounted as he talked to Gonzales and other local people. He realized that man had far outstripped the coyote as the turtles' worst enemy, and that the nesting population had been seriously depleted in the few years since it was photographed by Herrera. Although the sale of eggs was forbidden by Mexican law, turtles still were often robbed of their eggs while they were being laid, or immediately afterwards.

Over the millenia, turtles had evolved to cope with their natural predators. The Rancho Nuevo ridleys had found a remote nesting beach bordered by extensive lagoons that hindered the access of coyotes, skunks, opossums, raccoons and coatis. They nested in large numbers simultaneously, producing so many eggs, and subsequently so many hatchlings, that their predators were overwhelmed. Many hatchlings were able to survive because their enemies had lost interest in them as food. Now all of this had changed.

"The degree of exploitation of turtle eggs was too great to allow the species to survive," said Hildebrand. "I calculated conservatively that men destroyed 80 to 90 per cent of the nests from the arribada of June 25 on the same day they were constructed. If what I was told was correct, perhaps as many as 14,000 nests were robbed of eggs and the eggs sold. Estimates I heard of eggs taken from the first arribada of the year varied from 'a few used by ranchers for food' to '20 to 24 truckloads of 80,000 eggs each, going to the markets nearby."

The eggs reputedly sold for 50 centavos apiece in inland cities, where they were valued as an aphrodisiac. With regard to the slaughter of turtles, some reports said that only coastal inhabitants ate the meat, and others that the oil was prized more highly than the meat because it could be used as a remedy for lung and skin diseases, as well as for cooking when people couldn't afford lard.

Hildebrand and Carr, together with Tom Harrisson, another turtle biologist of international stature, advocated that the Mexican government should protect the eggs and hatchlings at Rancho Nuevo, and decided to make other biologists and conservationists throughout the world aware of the ridleys' plight before they were completely destroyed.

IV Overland With The Egg Convoys

DEARL ADAMS, a prominent Brownsville building contractor, saw a copy of the nesting film when it was borrowed from Herrera by a fellow member of the Brownsville Sportsmen Club. The film aroused a great deal of interest in the club and, after he had become the club's next president, Adams decided to try to establish a new colony of ridley turtles on South Padre Island, thirty miles up the coast from Brownsville. He and his wife Ethel planned to take eggs from Rancho Nuevo and incubate them in the sand at the similarly remote and desolate Padre Island.

It was not a minor undertaking. Now that they are both elderly, comfortable and retired, it is fairly difficult to picture them setting out on a mission that not only would anticipate most of the intensive and costly, government-sponsored, conservation work that was to come, but would require them to make long, uncomfortable drives over almost non-existent roads, and camp for weeks at a time on remote stretches of desolate coastline with next to nothing in the way of civilized amenities, solely for the purpose of transplanting a few turtle eggs. There is also the problem that members of sportsmen's clubs in Texas are supposed to confine their preservation efforts to respectable game animals.

"We are mostly hunters and fishermen, but first and foremost we are conservationist," Adams avows.

After he read an article by Carr entitled *The Riddle of the Ridley*, Adams had his wife Ethel go to the library to search for more information about turtles, and she found a book by Carr describing his research on green turtles in Costa Rica. Adams then talked to Hildebrand about the 500 baby green turtles Hildebrand was transplanting at the north end of Padre Island, and this led him to contact Francis McDonald at the Mexican fishing camp.

Late in the 1963 nesting season, McDonald sent him 98 ridley eggs by air. Some of these eggs were given to Joe Bruer, a Texas Parks and

Wildlife biologist, for what turned out to be an unsuccessful incubation, and the rest were buried in the sandhills at Padre Island. Although the eggs came carefully packed in a box of sand, the Adamses did not know how long they had been in the sand before being dug up or how they had been handled. During incubation they opened the nest several times to ensure that the eggs were still there, and only later realized that this was a mistake. When they finally dug up the nest it was swarming with sand crabs. All that remained were a few pieces of shell, fifty-eight worm-filled eggs, and two eggs holding partly-developed embryos.

For the next four years of their effort the Adamses were helped by local people who owned rugged vehicles that could cope with the often-flooded cattle track leading to the Rancho Nuevo beach. Ila Loetscher, a small, white-haired widow who in later years would become better known as the Turtle Lady of Padre Island, drove a little red beach-buggy in the convoys of 1965 and '66. Convoy members camped at Rancho Nuevo for up to two weeks while they collected eggs. Later, when hatching time approached, the Adamses set up camp for a further two weeks or more at Padre Island. Hildebrand visited the Padre Island camp several times as an interested observer.

Disappointed but not discouraged by the poor results in 1963, Adams planned ahead for 1964. He wrote to McDonald and Herrera to find out the best time to catch an arribada and was told that it would be from about April 27 to May 5. Then he obtained a permit from the U.S. Department of Agriculture to import some Mexican sand, and drove to Rancho Nuevo with four other club members and Joe Bruer in two 4-wheel drive pickups.

"The beach was patrolled day and night by Mexicans on foot and on horseback, on donkeys and on bicycles, waiting for the turtles," he said. "Sometimes an egg-collector would come by with a sack of eggs taken from an early arrival and offer to give or sell them to us. We declined as these eggs were usually in poor condition after being handled roughly and sometimes washed, thrown into a sack and bounced along on a horse or donkey."

The local people were friendly and helpful when they learned what the Adamses and their colleagues were trying to accomplish. The president of one ranch even offered them the use of his shower, which unfortunately was located three miles from the beach. They were told that, because of the severe droughts of the early sixties, the fish-filled lagoons behind the beach had dried up and fishermen had turned to turtles for a living. Turtle numbers had decreased greatly in recent years. The local people said that buyers came from Tampico and Mexico City every year, establishing camps at the beach and leaving with truck-loads of eggs for markets in the cities, and that boats would lie offshore and scoop up

*Ethel, Dearl and Darwal Adams
with friend outside their camp.*

thousands of live turtles so they could be cut open just for the eggs. The locals told Adams that they rarely ate turtle meat — Adams thought this was probably because they didn't have refrigeration.

The party waited nine days, saw only two turtles, and collected three hundred and fifty eggs. They heard later that an arribada occurred three days after they left. Forty-two days after transplanting the eggs to Padre Island, the Adamses set up their beach camp again, and this time they built a barrier around the nests to trap any hatchlings.

"On the fifty-sixth day we were rewarded with the appearance of one baby turtle," says Adams, smiling at the memory. "We were certain that it was the promise of more to come. I could hardly make myself leave the beach that day and drive the thirty-six miles to work, and I might just as well have stayed for all the good I was at the office."

Four more turtles were in the enclosure when they woke up next morning. The turtle watchers were elated, and Adams decided that there was no point at all in going to the office. He left the beach only to take one of the hatchlings to a photographer. Next day there were fifteen turtles in the enclosure.

"Fifteen little turtles fighting like mad to get to the water look like twice as many," Adams says. "We had a lot of fun watching them race to the surf about seventy-five yards away. We tried to protect them from sand crabs that were waiting all along their path, but still two were killed before they got to the water. We saw the crabs going for them, and arrived about the same time, but not before they had punctured the turtles' necks with their claws."

Heat and flies drove them from the beach on the twentieth day. More hatchlings may have appeared after they left.

Partly as a result of publicity in several Texas newspapers, the convoy grew to six 4-wheel drive vehicles in 1965. This year, like all the others, was very disappointing as far as seeing a lot of turtles on the beach was concerned. Convoy members had to be content with collecting eight hundred and fifty eggs from scattered nests.

Sand crab with its claws on the throat of a hatchling.

"The surf was full of turtles and we could see heads sticking out in all directions near the end of our sixteen-day stay, when most of the others had left," says Adams. "We watched by the hour, expecting them all to come out of the water, but they never did — just a few at a time now and again. The Hoyts stayed on almost to the end of their thirty-day visas and still did not see the migration."

The Adamses transplanting technique was by now quite sophisticated. They wore cotton gloves to keep the eggs clean and tried to move the nests intact, together with the surrounding sand soaked with laying fluids, into their Styrofoam boxes. The eggs from each nest were layered in their own sand and separated from those of the next nest by paper towels.

At Padre Island the holes scooped out of the sand by hand were jug-shaped, "as nearly as possible the same as mamma dug", and eggs from different nests were transplanted separately. The nursery enclosure was more and more heavily fortified every year in an effort to protect the hatchlings from coyotes and sand crabs.

In 1965, coyotes dug up three of the nests and prowled around the enclosure at night, and the iron stakes marking the positions of the nests were pulled up by a passerby whose motivation remains obscure. Again distressed by heat and flies in the house trailer, the family moved out. When Adams returned to break camp, forty-nine days after burying the eggs, he found twenty hatchlings scurrying about in the enclosure. Although the sand was torn up and there were coyote tracks everywhere, several more hatchlings appeared on succeeding mornings. One night he slept armed in the back of his pickup truck, ready to repulse a coyote attack but, although they woke him with their prowling, he saw only their tracks.

His wife and three-year-old son and their convoy friends, the Lucious Palmers, were there when the next seventeen hatched. The Palmers had been with them the whole time at Rancho Nuevo and these were the first hatchlings they had seen. Their reaction, as described by Adams, seems to be typical:

"Lou was everywhere, helping them over the barriers and moving them closer to the water, and talking all the time to them in baby talk. I told him I thought they gained strength by their hard struggle to get to the water, but he still insisted on helping them when the going got tough."

"Whenever we went to Rancho Nuevo I urged the local people to ask their government to start some kind of conservation program," says Adams, "and in 1966 I made the trip to Mexico City to talk to the Director-General of the Department of Commerce. He gave me his support and a permit to export 2000 eggs."

In 1966 a convoy of six vehicles collected 2,102 eggs. The Adamses planted them in thirteen nests inside a wire cage to protect them from coyotes and sand crabs. Only fifty-four hatched.

The big breakthrough came in 1967 when, for the first time, the eggs were spared the rough journey overland. That year two thousand eggs were flown to Padre Island and transplanted into eighteen nests. Amid great jubilation, about fifty people, members of the convoy and their families, escorted 1,102 hatchlings to the sea. This meant that over five years they had watched a total of 1,227 hatchlings swim into the Gulf of Mexico.

"Some hatchlings from each year were given to Ila Loetscher for a growth study in her aquarium, so we would know how long they took to reach maturity and therefore when to expect them back," Adams says. "She had devoted her knowledge, time, and money to providing a way station for sick and injured turtles, which were constantly being brought to her for care."

The Adamses waited to see whether any of their hatchlings would return to nest at Padre Island. Seven years after the first transplanted eggs hatched, a ridley they called Alpha nested on the South Padre Island beach. One hatchling from this nest broke through its shell on July 4th and was called Yankee Doodle Dandy. Nobody knows whether Alpha, or the other five ridleys recorded nesting at Padre Island since then, were once convoy hatchlings, because sporadic nestings of Kemp's ridleys on Padre Island are known to have occurred previously.

The Adamses long-term plan, if more turtles returned to Padre Island, was to tag them, transplant their eggs to an enclosed, protected area, and count and protect the hatchlings. They also intended to return to Rancho Nuevo for more eggs with which to augment the colony.

"All the conservation work was done without any outside grants or help, at convoy members' expense," Adams comments. "However, if more turtles had returned, we would have approached government agencies in an effort to get the nesting area at Padre Island closed to vehicular traffic in the nesting season. Traffic along the beach, especially at weekends, was so great that we were afraid that the turtles might be frightened away, even if they wanted to return."

The National Wildlife Foundation, the Sears-Roebuck Foundation, and Sportsmen Clubs of Texas jointly presented Dearl Adams with their Wildlife Conservationist of the Year Award at a banquet in Austin during 1966. Newspaper reports mention that Ethel received a special "Baby Turtle Sitter of the Year" award, because of the time she spent guarding the nests on Padre Island while her husband checked up on his contracting business.

V Coyote Patrol Superseded

IN 1966 THE CONVOY MEMBERS discovered that the Mexican government had begun to protect the turtles at Rancho Nuevo. When they arrived, Mexican Marines were patrolling the beach and commercial trading in eggs had been stopped. Biologists René Márquez and Humberto Chávez were busy tagging and measuring the nesting turtles and transplanting eggs to a central, fenced-in corral where they could be guarded throughout incubation.

Two years after Hildebrand's plea for conservation measures to save the Kemp's ridley from extinction, the Estación de Biologia Pesquera (Marine Biology Station) had been established at Tampico. Part of its joint program with two government agencies and the naval authorities of the area was to study the Kemp's ridley and develop a plan to protect it.

"Their program was much more thorough and scientific than ours has been," Adams wrote in 1966 in the *International Turtle and Tortoise Society Journal.*[7] "Among other things they measured the depth of each nest and replanted the eggs at the same depth as they were dug out. They also had an exact record of when they were laid."

Chávez, Martin Contreras and Eduardo Hernandez described their 1966 conservation program at Rancho Nuevo in a landmark paper[8] which was reprinted in translation as *On the Coast of Tamaulipas* in the *International Turtle and Tortoise Society Journal* in 1968. They quoted Hildebrand's 1963 paper at length, described Adams' project, and told how a camp had been established in the nesting area for the staff of biologists, fishery inspectors, and Marines from the Naval Base at Tampico, to obtain biological data, protect the eggs and hatchlings, and tag nesting turtles.

The biologists observed seven arribadas, the largest numbering 1,500 turtles. They noted that all the arrivals took place in moderate to strong winds, that only two coincided with the beginning of a full moon, that some of the turtles nested three times in a season, and that the average number of eggs in the nests was 110. They made continuous patrols along twenty miles of beach, covering the six miles around Rancho Nuevo twice a day, and transplanted almost 30,000 eggs into a central corral guarded by Marines. Two inspectors and four marine officers kept the vigil set up by the Dirección de Pesca, travelling six miles twice a day over the beach near Rancho Nuevo. When an arribada occurred, they remained on guard day and night for the first forty-eight hours. After two days in the sand the eggs developed dark brown or black spots and people no longer considered them edible. Nor, apparently, did the coyotes.

"Each person was allowed to extract eggs from only one nest," wrote the biologists. "We had to arrest only two persons, who were caught with thousands of eggs each. In general, the people of Rancho Nuevo conformed to the prohibition against disturbing the nests, a resolution applied for the first time in the area. We feel that in 1966, 90% of the nests suffered no damage."

Trucks belonging to seven businessmen arrived around the end of April to transport eggs to market, but drove away empty. Local people told the biologists that in 1965 the price of turtle eggs had been 5 centavos apiece at markets in Tampico, Poza Rica and Mexico City.

"We recorded the date and the time of the hatching of 1,664 Lepidochelys kempi... We could not determine exactly the number of turtles hatched from the transplanted eggs because we had not foreseen the need for wire fences around each nest to impede the immediate trip to the sea of the hatchlings," the biologists wrote. "Several times when we arrived at the transplanting zone the hatchlings had already left their nests, so we could not record their number, the hour of hatching, or the nest from which they came."

Most of the hatchlings recorded appeared between 5 and 7 a.m., after 53 to 56 days of incubation. The range of incubation times was from 50 to 70 days, compared with Adams' figures of approximately 50 to 60 days.

The biologists mounted a campaign against some of the main predators on land — the sand crab, coyote, blackbird and vulture. At sea, the hatchlings' worst enemies were the white sea bass and the jurel (yellow jack) fish. Eleven newly hatched ridleys were found in the stomach of one white sea-bass caught nearby.

"The number of nesting females that arrive at Rancho Nuevo area has diminished considerably during the past few years because of the immoderate extraction of eggs. But with permanent protective measures, already initiated in 1966, we are confident we can enlarge their numbers," the biologists concluded. "We consider that one of the most effective measures of protection will be the construction of a place for breeding turtles with an adequate pond where the young specimens would be confined for at least three months, thereby increasing the percentage of survival."

A Mexican emptying hundreds of hatchlings along the shore.

VI Difficult Times

IN CONTRAST TO the fine efforts of many Mexican biologists and conservationists, some people in Mexico were bent on gaining financially from the turtles. The Mexican government of the time, which did not subscribe to the present government's excellent conservation policies, was willing to help them.

Dr. Peter Pritchard has good reason to remember the events of that period. After coming from Oxford, England, to be one of Carr's graduate students, he drove his Land Rover to Rancho Nuevo a number of times in the late 1960's and early 1970's to assist the Mexican efforts to save the ridleys. Pritchard is now Senior Vice-President of the Florida Audubon Society and author of the standard work *Encyclopaedia of Turtles*. He has been described to the author as tall, friendly, outgoing, perceptive, and having an interesting British accent. He is also very erudite and articulate, especially on the subject of turtles:

"I arrived at the beach in 1970 to find that cement was being poured for a new facility of some kind, right beside the sea. A considerable number of workers were in evidence and their vehicles bore license plates from the State of Colima, hundreds of miles away on the Pacific coast. At first I was told that this was a fish-processing plant, but before long it became clear that it was to be a slaughterhouse for Kemp's ridleys. The man in charge claimed to have a permit from Mexico City allowing the taking of 2,000 adult ridleys for industrial purposes (skins and meat)."

Since this figure corresponded roughly to the known world population of adult female Kemp's ridleys at the time, and the building was being erected on the only known mass nesting site for the species, there was a serious possibility that nearly every adult Kemp's ridley in existence might be killed. Nobody could produce the actual permit, so Pritchard drove to Mexico City to ask the Subsecretaria de Industria y Comercio what was going on.

In Mexico City he was courteously received and shown a copy of the permit. It specified that male turtles could be taken at sea, at a maximum rate of fifty per day, for the month of May. If, however, this proved difficult or impossible, and males were not available in the numbers needed, females could be taken instead. These females could be taken off the beach if they could not be caught at sea and, if it turned out to be difficult to get fifty each day, they could be taken according to any daily schedule that the turtle-butchers devised.

"The government representatives told me that the permit had been issued 'experimentally' in response to industry pressure and they invited me to send in any comments I might have," Pritchard recalls. "I sent them in immediately and broadcast the disastrous development to members of the turtle conservation community as soon as possible. Telegrams soon started to arrive from as far away as Borneo and South Africa, and high-level interventions were launched by such dignitaries as Prince Philip and Charles Lindbergh. No heads rolled in Mexico, but much embarrassment was felt and my lack of diplomatic restraint was the source of a lot of complaints."

By happy chance, the turtles were saved by the lateness of the arribada that year. Pritchard comments that those associated with the slaughterhouse venture were unaccustomed to long sojourns on remote beaches and did not wait for it to arrive. No doubt the coolness of the reception at Rancho Nuevo also contributed to their early departure. Only about four turtles were actually slaughtered, and the government concluded that the 'experimental harvest' had been unsuccessful and should not be repeated.

"But a very slightly different turn of events could have resulted in the legal killing of virtually all adult female Kemp's ridleys in the world in the course of a single month," Pritchard notes.

Dr. René Márquez Millan[9] is the most outstanding of the Mexican ridley conservationists and the person directly responsible for the conservation effort at Rancho Nuevo. He is short, slight and very youthful-looking, even though he is now in his mid-forties and his black hair and moustache have begun to be tinged with grey. He has what is described as a colorful and adequate command of English. Enormous dedication is the basic requirement for his position as Chief of Turtle Conservation for Mexico's Instituto Nacional de la Pesca, a position which in the past has been beset with political difficulties. For over twenty years, turtles were a political football in Mexico, because businessmen and exploiters had a great deal of influence in government. Recently, the tide has turned in favor of the turtles: in 1987, President Miguel de la Madrid named sixteen nesting beaches as sea turtle sanctuaries. In the mid-sixties, Márquez visited Archie Carr's camp at Tortuguero, in Costa Rica, to learn the basic

René Márquez helps attach a satellite tag to a female ridley at Rancho Nuevo.

techniques of beach patrolling for turtles and tagging, so he could get the Mexican Kemp's ridley program under way. He and Pritchard met for the first time when they worked together on Rancho Nuevo beach in 1967.

In a 1973 paper,[10] Márquez and Pritchard warned that the demand for turtle leather, though diminishing, was still high and that in recent years commercial establishments had made strong overtures to the Mexican government for permission to kill nesting ridleys on the beach for their skins. They also noted that, as the commercial importance of the turtle decreased, it was becoming harder for conservation crews to obtain adequate funds for protection of the breeding colony. They deplored the organized capture of ridleys at sea, which was concentrated at Cedar Key, Florida, where the catch almost entirely comprised immature turtles, and at Campeche, Mexico, where adult turtles were taken. They reminded readers that many conservationists had recommended to the United States government that the species should be completely protected.

"Probably the most serious problem of all, however, and the hardest to control, is the accidental capture and drowning of ridleys in shrimp trawls and, to a lesser extent, shark nets, particularly as they migrate to and from the nesting grounds," they concluded.

The problem of accidental capture in shrimp trawls, which has not diminished in importance, is one that we shall return to more than once in this book.

VII International Action

HILDEBRAND, CARR AND PRITCHARD, who led the Turtle Working Group of the International Union for the Conservation of Nature and Natural Resources, were interested in Pritchard's idea of using United States volunteers to bolster the Mexican beach patrols. They had been observing Mexico's ridley conservation effort closely, and had begun to draw the problem to the attention of people around the world, in the process arousing the interest of biologists working in three different agencies of the federal government.

The National Park Service (NPS) requested the late Dr. Howard ("Duke") Campbell, research biologist with the U.S. Fish and Wildlife Service (FWS) to study the feasibility of establishing a nesting colony of sea turtles at Padre Island, and also asked the advice of Jack Woody, Chief of the Endangered Species Office (South-west Region) of the FWS. Woody, now in his fifties, is tall, thin and wiry, with brown hair, a short beard and the weatherbeaten face of a long-time outdoorsman. In his senior position he could, if he wished, spend the rest of his working days behind a desk, but he remains a hands-on biologist and has rarely if ever been observed to wear a suit and tie. He is also a gifted raconteur. One of his most effective current roles is as a problem solver working face-to-face with key people on the Mexican side of the program.

"We suggested that we concentrate on the Kemp's ridley, making a ten-year agreement with Mexico to exchange eggs for conservation assistance on the beach." Woody says. The two agencies of the U.S. Department of the Interior decided to do this and invited the National Marine Fisheries Service (NMFS) and the Texas Parks and Wildlife Department (TPWD) to cooperate. For the first time, members of NPS, FWS and NMFS agreed to work together on a single project and in 1977, together with Márquez, they drew up an international action plan which has guided the program ever since.

INTERNATIONAL CONSERVATION PLAN

The four people mainly responsible for putting the plan into effect were all biologists in government service. They were Márquez, who was now Chief of Turtle Conservation for Mexico's Department of Fisheries (Instituto Nacional de la Pesca, often referred to simply as Pesca); Jack Woody, now National Sea Turtle Co-ordinator for the FWS; Dr. Milford Fletcher, Chief Scientist of the NPS (Southwest Region), and Dr. Edward Klima, Director of the Galveston Laboratory, NMFS. Jim Woods, Biologist with the NPS (Padre Island National Seashore — PAIS) and a former student of Hildebrand, headed the incubation-hatching-imprinting phase of Operation Head Start at Padre Island. Robert Whistler, Chief Naturalist and now Chief of Interpretation with the NPS (PAIS), provided major assistance throughout the program. Dr. James McVey, Chief of the Aquaculture Division, NMFS, led the head start work at the Galveston Laboratory.

Under the new program:

• Further efforts would be made to prohibit the possession and sale of eggs, turtles and various turtle products, all of which were in great demand. (Kemp's ridley was listed in the species covered by the United States Endangered Species Act of 1973, and protected from harvesting for food and leather. Mexico declared Rancho Nuevo beach to be a natural reserve in 1977, and continued to increase the protection of eggs and turtles that had begun in 1966.)

• Mexican Marines, and an international team of biologists, would continue to patrol the beach and protect nesting turtles, nests, eggs and hatchlings from April through August or September, and the biologists would continue the work of tagging nesting turtles and transferring clutches of eggs to protected corrals. Major responsibility for scientific studies would rest with the Mexicans, while the Americans would provide field support services and assist with all aspects of the conservation program.

• The use of turtle excluder devices (TEDs, also called trawling efficiency devices) on shrimp trawls would be promoted. These devices are designed to allow turtles and finfish to escape from shrimp trawls after they have been captured unintentionally. The National Marine Fisheries Service undertook to develop an acceptable TED that would not reduce the performance of the trawl as a catcher of shrimp.

• The area in front of the Rancho Nuevo Beach would continue to be a 'no-trawl' zone.

Box continued

• The Operation Head Start project would attempt to establish a second nesting colony of Kemp's ridleys at the Padre Island National Seashore. Two thousand eggs would be collected annually for ten years by a team comprising biologists from Pesca together with a field crew organized by the United States Fish and Wildlife Service and the Florida Audubon Society (succeeded, after the first three years, by the Gladys Porter Zoo). The head start eggs would be incubated at the National Seashore in Padre Island sand by the National Park Service, and the hatchlings would crawl down the beach to the sea at Padre Island before being recaptured and taken to the Galveston Laboratory of the National Marine Fisheries Service's Southeast Fisheries Center. At Galveston they would be raised in a sheltered environment for the first, most hazardous, ten months of their lives, before being released into the Gulf of Mexico. The Texas Parks and Wildlife Department would also assist with the project. At all stages of the project, marine biologists would experiment with and do research into imprinting and head starting.

Mexican and U.S. personnel bury eggs in a guarded corral. Pat Burchfield and a student from Tampico's Universidad del Noreste bend over a facsimile nest in the foreground.

The International team delivers nests to a corral during an arribada.

From 1978 onwards, biologists from Mexico, the United States and various other countries have lived in a 'turtle camp' at Rancho Nuevo with international support personnel, and worked together for the five-month nesting and hatching season. Each year the Fish and Wildlife Service provides funding for a group of marine biologists, marine biology graduate students working for advanced degrees, and biology students from the U.S. to go to Mexico with vehicles and equipment to assist with the project. The bulk of the work at the camp is in fact rather routine, consisting as it does of making daily patrols to look for turtle tracks and nests and to collect eggs and return them to a protected corral, but it does have its exciting moments. The U.S. participants emphasize that this is a Mexican project, in a Mexican wildlife sanctuary, and that the U.S. role is to assist. A Mexican biologist is in overall charge of all of the biological work done at the camp.

Pritchard led the United States field team for the first three years (1978-80). Initially all of the U.S. biologists except Pritchard and Duke Campbell were from the University of Central Florida. In 1979 a Mexican citizen, veterinarian Georgita Ruiz, was one of the United States contingent of six. That year the Mexican personnel comprised four biologists, two Fisheries Inspectors, Manuel Sánchez Perez the camp manager, two technicians/camp helpers, and the Marine contingent of a sergeant and four privates. In addition, two Dutch biologists, Han van Dissel and Ariane van Schravendijk, were engaged directly by the Mexicans to construct a population model for the species on the basis of long-term data on tag returns for Rancho Nuevo ridleys. The team collected data on the condition and behavior of the turtles, tagged them, gathered the Operation Head Start eggs, moved the other eggs into man-made nests in protected corrals or, less frequently, into Styrofoam hatching boxes, kept a count of the hatchlings being released, and recorded meteorological data for the site.

HILDEBRAND BATTLES ON

"The nesting colony at Rancho Nuevo is now getting so small that we should try to develop any small, isolated nesting group of Kemp's ridleys," says Professor Hildebrand, who at 65 is still actively doing field work on sea turtles. Last year he spent some of his three and a half months in Mexico trying to save one such colony. His daughter Gabrielle, who is an artist, sometimes accompanies him on his trips to Mexico.

"I have written a paper on the small group of ten to thirty turtles that nest individually on a 20 km stretch of coast at Tecolutla, 110 miles north of Veracruz. One fisheries inspector of Pesca, with some Mexican government assistance, has already put a lot of effort into trying to preserve that little nesting colony and recovers up to twenty nests a year. I have been making a reconnaissance survey and trying to work through the NMFS and the FWS to obtain financial help for the colony from the U.S. government."

As a result, the FWS is supplying a three-wheeled motor-cycle, together with other assistance, so the inspector can protect many more nests than was possible on foot. On the basis of Hildebrand's recommendations, the FWS will investigate another small reported nesting ground in the State of Veracruz and work with Pesca to try to get university students to work there.

Hildebrand also visited the Yucatan three times during the year, trying to obtain improved protection for two nesting colonies of hawksbills. Again he is trying to start a cooperative program between the Mexicans, who have done the previous work there, and the Americans.

Jack Woody in action, transplanting eggs.

Because of the continuing decline in the number of nesting turtles, the number of nests collected and translocated to corrals fell from 834 to 672 between 1978 and 1986. The number of hatchlings released did not show a corresponding decrease over the same period because of the team's improved egg collection and hatching techniques. A total of 48,009 hatchlings from 85,217 eggs made their way to the sea in 1978, compared with about 48,950 from 65,258 eggs in 1986.

VIII Early Days

As a direct outcome of the new cooperative turtle program, the Mexican Army captured Jack Woody, two U.S. Coast Guard aircraft and about fifteen sailors, and held them for two days in 1978.

"We were just getting started and we didn't have much money, so we got the Coast Guard at Corpus Christi to volunteer to go down to collect the eggs and hatchlings from Rancho Nuevo," Woody explains. "I told the commander that I would get the permits to export the eggs and I asked him to make the necessary arrangements for the plane."

Woody arrived at Corpus Christi Airport expecting to find a small aircraft appropriate for transporting turtle eggs. Instead, a large military helicopter and a huge, twin-engined Convair "which holds about sixty people" were both being readied to depart. He tried without success to persuade the commander to take only the helicopter.

"When I boarded the plane I found there were about fifteen enlisted sailors and officers sitting in it," says Woody. "They told me they were making the trip to get extra flight pay. I assumed they knew where they were going. I didn't find out until later that they had just got on board without asking. So we all took off for Tampico, giving the helicopter an hour's start.

"As we taxied towards the terminal at Tampico to refuel, we suddenly noticed military trucks full of armed soldiers driving towards us. The trucks stopped and all the soldiers jumped out and surrounded the plane in a menacing way. I'll never forget the expression on the face of one of our sailors when he woke up, looked out the window, and saw all the weapons. He jumped right out of his seat and said 'Oh, my God! Where are we?' For all he knew we could have been in Cuba or Nicaragua, or maybe Lebanon. When I looked across the tarmac I saw the helicopter in the same situation. Then I knew we had a problem — the aircraft were worth 20 or 30 million dollars and somebody would be upset."

The local military commander pointed out that proper clearance had not been obtained for the aircraft, and Woody braced himself for what would be two long days of tedious argument with various kinds of officialdom.

"The sailors and officers had no money or belongings other than the fatigue outfits they were wearing," Woody recalls. "I had a credit card. I had to pay for meals and accommodation for half the United States Navy and Ed Smith, an NMFS special agent we had aboard, for two days. My VISA bill was pretty high that month.

"In the meantime, word was getting back that property and personnel of the United States had been seized by the Mexican government and people were being held against their will. The Secretary of the Interior, the Defense Department and the Department of State all became involved in negotiations with various entities of the Mexican government.

"I called my wife and found she'd been getting phone calls from all over the world. One of them was from the Director of the Fish and Wildlife Service in Washington. He just said to her, his voice cracking —

'Where the hell is Woody?'

'I don't know,' she replied. 'I haven't seen him in a week.'"

After two nights of playing host to the sailors in Tampico, Woody was given a clearance by the comandante. He was told he could leave for Rancho Nuevo, but that he could collect only eggs, and not eggs and hatchlings as specified by his permit. He decided not to argue any further and left in the helicopter. Evidently the turtles had the last word, because a number of eggs seem to have hatched during the flight home from the sanctuary. There were plenty of broken shells in the boxes to prove it.

"When I got back I had to write pages of explanation to various people in the United States government. Some thought it was funny and some were mad because it did create something of an international incident," Woody says placidly. "But we got the job done."

"In those days we had to deal with emergencies as best we could. Sometimes, when the camp at Rancho Nuevo was isolated by flooding, we ran out of food and had to eat cacti and armadillos — believe me, they taste very good when you're hungry. Once a Marine drank too much liquor and stopped breathing. My daughter gave him mouth-to-mouth resuscitation, and then a bunch of Mexicans took him off to try to find a doctor."

At first the field crew often swam at the beach without worrying about sharks, though Woody told them he had seen large hammerheads just beyond the breakers when he flew overhead. Then one day a Mexican tourist on a motorbike ran over a nesting turtle and smashed its shell.

"The Marines grabbed him and carted him off — for all we know, maybe they shot him," Woody says.

When they had finished dissecting the dead turtle, the biologists left the carcass near the water, and were disturbed to notice next morning that the ocean nearby was full of sharks, with large fins sticking out of waves in the shallows. That ended the swimming.

Peter Pritchard and his son Dominic watch a nesting turtle.

IX Interesting Times

THE TEAM HAD TO WORK until midnight to finish moving the nests from a major arribada, as Pritchard reported when he was principal investigator for a U.S. Fish and Wildlife Contract that provided support for the joint conservation program from 1978 to 1980.[11] Typically, at such times the wind strength was sufficient to collapse tents and lead to confusion and multilingual imprecations in the darkness. Sometimes there was also a violent rainstorm which, as well as augmenting the already over-generous supply of mud, was liable to create additional work by stimulating the emergence of new hatchlings in the corrals. The numbers of hatchlings produced in 1978 and 1979 were 48,000 and 64,000; the hatchling yields from Operation Head Start eggs in those years were 88 and 86 percent.

"The joint program appears to be very successful." he wrote. "After one season, even those without previous speaking knowledge of Spanish develop sufficient ability with the language for basic communication — very important when a major arribada comes ashore and a highly coordinated effort by all Mexican and U.S. personnel is needed. Ability to speak Spanish is, of course, a major desideratum; but perhaps more important are a positive attitude, physical toughness and sustained enthusiasm."

".....both Richard Byles and Tim Clabaugh worked for several seasons on loggerhead turtle patrols on Merritt Island, Florida, before joining the Rancho Nuevo team in 1978. Both have extensive knowledge of mechanics and vehicle repair that proves fully as necessary for the project as the knowledge of turtles."

There were a variety of problems. Political and bureaucratic difficulties in Mexico obstructed Pesca and ensured that its financial support was generally both inadequate and late. The demanding beach conditions caused too much time to be spent keeping vehicles in working order and at Pritchard's suggestion several three-wheeled motorized tricyles were bought. These ensured that beach patrols were thorough and regular, that most of the eggs were transplanted, and that a good proportion of the nesting turtles were tagged and measured. It became obvious that another three-wheeler was needed.

The entry for May 26 in Pritchard's diary reads: "Poachers' butchery site was found, 6.2 miles south of camp near the lagoon. Clearly the meat from these turtles had been transported away by boat."

May 28: "Byles visited the beach north of San Vincente and found eight nests in seven miles, all but two of which had been robbed. Tracks of a horse led up to each of the eight nests. The nests had been rearranged to look undisturbed, but the horse tracks were not obscured in any way."

Up to a hundred nests were being taken each year by poachers. Signs needed to be posted warning that the taking of eggs and turtles was prohibited and explaining why. The signs should be accompanied by warnings about the penalties for disobeying the prohibition and by education in the surrounding communities about the need for conservation.

Diary entries mention the camp's visitors, who included Márquez, Hildebrand, Woody, and Daniel Rios Olmeda, and reflect the primitive living conditions:

April 20: "Tents set up and vehicles checked out. New concrete block permanent buildings partially constructed."

May 17: "Construction of egg house started — 7x4 meter floor plan, palm thatch walls and tar paper roof. Inside lined with plastic to stop the wind and keep heat in."

May 18: "Egg house completed."

May 19: "Pritchard and family and Burchfield arrived just after midnight; truck had broken down just the other side of Rancho Nuevo."

May 24: "Both trucks broke down but were repaired."

June 4: "Pritchard and family attempted to leave camp in the Dodge Power Wagon but were prevented by extensive mud following two days of rain........"

June 6: "Pritchard went across the lagoon by boat, with the Honda, and drove up the beach to get a truck to bring the other two and the equipment...."

June 10: "The rain prompted the emergence of the first hatchlings in the corral. Several tents collapsed and general confusion in camp."

The beach could be reached by truck only in dry weather. When it rained, the land flooded quickly, and the river mouths or 'barras' about ten miles north and south of the camp became waist-deep and had to be crossed by wading or rafting.

"At Rancho Nuevo we often wonder what is going on just over the horizon," reads one plaintive entry in Pritchard's report. He made a strong case for a light aircraft to be stationed at the camp in future seasons. The plane would be useful for patrolling the beach north and south of the barras, evacuating personnel in emergencies, transporting eggs to Padre Island, and harassing poachers.

A large team was needed to cope with arribadas and with protecting eggs on the beach from natural predators, poachers, erosion or flooding. Eggs in the egg house needed less protection, but it would be too costly to incubate the majority of the eggs in boxes, and such an incubation could have undesirable effects on the sex ratios of hatchlings and possibly interfere with natural imprinting. After studying the temperatures in natural and box nests, Pritchard advised that the egg house should be thoroughly insulated and heated. The box nests would then be as well insulated from extremes of temperature as natural nests buried on the beach.

The biologists would continue to make do with tents, which would give them favorable opportunities to make the acquaintance of other inhabitants of the site. Informal reports mention boa constrictors in the kitchen, black widow spiders in the toilet, and large tropical rattlesnakes beside the beach trikes.

X Troubled Waters

IN THE SUMMER OF 1979, at a time when the nesting season was essentially over and the only member of the U.S. contingent remaining on the beach was biologist Richard Byles, the hatchlings and their protectors found themselves at the centre of a major crisis. Crude oil from the blowout of the IXTOC 1 oil well in the Gulf of Campeche, which occurred in the spring of that year, was being carried in a north-westerly direction across the Gulf, missing the south-west Mexican Gulf coast and coming ashore in Tamaulipas and Texas. In a glare of international publicity, preparations were made to evacuate the season's hatchlings from Rancho Nuevo by helicopter. Byles, a young, rugged, bearded outdoorsman, who has since acquired a Ph.D. and a job with the U.S. Fish and Wildlife Service, was the right man on the spot.

The contingency plan, devised by Woody and Pritchard when the oil slick first began to move up the coast, was that, if oil came ashore at Rancho Nuevo, the hatchlings would be held in temporary containers after they emerged from the nests and air-lifted at intervals to oil-free parts of the Gulf for release. Arrangements for the use of helicopters were made with the U.S. Coast Guard and Woody obtained a letter formally requesting this assistance from the Director of Departamento de Pesca.

Some oil was observed on the beach on July 17, and Pesca officials who went on a reconnaissance flight reported isolated patches of oil at sea. Four days later, Byles noticed about twenty men erecting a floating oil barricade across the mouth of Barra del Tordo, by Campo Andrés, presumably to keep oil out of the oyster beds. On that same afternoon, globs of sticky oil appeared in the sea at the mouth of Barra Coma, the site of the turtle camp.

Construction of the temporary holding pens was begun next day in the lagoon at Barra del Tordo, nine miles south of the turtle camp. The amount of oil on the beach remained very small, although large surface slicks were present 80 to 120 miles off shore. Then, on July 25, high tides

Two crates of hatchlings hang from a helicopter over the sea.

breached the sandbar at the normally-closed entrance to the lagoon where the hatchlings were being held.

In case oil might enter the lagoon, 550 hatchlings were kept overnight in buckets and other improvised containers, just in time to be inspected by a group of visiting VIP's, including the Director of Pemex (the organization responsible for the oil spill), the Director of Aquaculture, the Comandante of the First Naval Zone, and a number of prominent Mexican citizens. They arrived by Pemex helicopter and a plan was announced for taking the hatchlings out to sea aboard a Pemex helicopter, rather than on one belonging to the U.S. Coast Guard. The visitors saw high tides bringing oil into the lagoon and a number of blue crabs lying dead on the beach, presumably from oil ingestion. They informed Byles of the cleanest nearby area for hatchling release but nobody knew whether there was any sargassum there for the turtles to hide in.

By this time the potential effect of the oil spill on the hatchling turtles had caught the attention of international news media. Television crews from Tampico, Los Angeles, and other places expressed interest and, together with representatives of newspapers and other news media, they arrived on the beach and interviewed Manuel Sánchez and Byles. On July 26 several trucks arrived unexpectedly at Barra Coma, bringing heavy equipment with which to construct floating barricades across the mouths of Barra Coma and Boca San Vincente, a river-mouth six miles north of the base camp.

A helicopter survey on July 27 showed that the amount of oil in the vicinity had diminished, and the area adjacent to Barra Coma appeared clean. A large raft of sargassum was identified in a clean area south-east of Barra del Tordo and this was designated as the first hatchling release area. It was decided to release the turtles just a little to the east of this weed patch, because it was possible that the downdraft from the helicopter might force them too deep into the sargassum and suffocate them.

For the release, two plastic crates of about 500 hatchlings each were suspended fifteen metres below the helicopter, with an extra line that could be pulled to capsize the hatchlings into the sea. And so on July 29, in the course of seven separate trips, 8,298 hatchlings were released. Some of them had been held for five days, but the total mortality during the holding period was only 225 turtles. Between the second and third flights an ABC news team arrived from Arlington, Texas, to share in the

A twin-engined plane in deep vegetation at Rancho Nuevo airstrip.

excitement. Helicopter flights on August 5, 13 and 21 released a further 5,286 hatchlings. A few nests that hatched shortly after the August 5 flight were set free directly into the ocean, because the mortality rate became too high if hatchlings were held for more than five days. Sixteen Styrofoam hatching boxes were taken to Tampico to complete their incubation; there too the hatchlings were released from a helicopter.

The arguments for having an aircraft bore fruit in 1980, and Pritchard's next job was to find a suitable landing place near the turtle camp. He and field workers marked off several hundred yards of a comparatively scrub-free stretch of duneland and dragged a heavy log up and down behind a pickup truck until, to quote Pritchard:

"... we thought we had done sufficient environmental damage to allow an aircraft to land.

"Then I drove to Brownsville to meet the pilot and escort him to the strip," he relates. At Brownsville he discovered that the first landing would be made not by the Florida Audubon Society's little Cessna, but by a sleek, twin-engined plane, property of the federal government.

"Hold it," Pritchard said nervously to the pilot, a dynamic individual by the name of Tug Kangus, "this thing will never land on our little strip, it's too big."

"How long is the strip?" asked Tug.

"About from here to there," Pritchard replied, waving his hands vaguely.

"No problem," said Tug.

Tug was used to taking off in the rarefied atmosphere of Albuquerque and felt that anything would be possible on a sea-level strip. Pritchard doubtfully agreed and off they went.

As they came in low over the turtle camp, camp personnel, both U.S. and Mexican, showed signs of alarm which evolved into emphatic gestures of "Don't do it!", "Impossible!", and so on, when they realised that the pilot intended to land.

Ignoring advice from the ground, they skimmed over a dry but soft-bottomed lake and cleared a four-foot barbed-wire fence by inches before touching down. Quite soon it became apparent that they would still have a lot of forward speed when they got to the end of the airstrip, so Tug veered off onto a donkey path where heavy brush dragged over the wings and buzz-sawed through the propellers, aiding deceleration. They ultimately came to a halt, unscathed and even proud of themselves, but it took a long time to pick all the vegetation out of the aircraft. The takeoff for the return journey was made, without further modification of the

"Car Coming!" as the Cessna taxis along a narrow road.

airstrip, after gunning the engines for some time and executing a 360° turn to gather momentum without using up any runway.

This was almost the last occasion on which a twin-engined plane attempted to land at the Rancho Nuevo international airstrip. (In 1986 a twin Beechcraft landed, got stuck in the mud, and barely made it off with Pat Burchfield and a coworker.) Subsequent landings were made by a small Cessna. Even with the Cessna it was necessary to shuttle people or equipment ten miles south to a straight stretch of highway if the load consisted of more than one or two people.

The usual Cessna pilot at this time was a Ms. Gray Bower, described by Pritchard as being safe but enterprising. She flew the Audubon plane initially, and later donated her own plane and flying time to the project. Tug Kangus had returned to the uncluttered open spaces of New Mexico, but takeoffs and landings continued to be unorthodox. Pritchard notes that on one occasion they taxied up to the little motel at Barra del Tordo and parked overnight in the parking lot without raising an eyebrow. The motel manager volunteered to hold up traffic for their takeoff in the morning. On another occasion a bus suddenly appeared, coming towards them over a slight rise in the road while they were still getting up speed to take off. Fortunately, the bus driver was alert and swerved into a ditch. There is no record of what he said at the time.

"We had a nearly comparable experience once at the U.S. end of our egg-shuttle flight. The pilot this time was the redoubtable Kim Cliffton, veteran of the Michoacan black turtle project. While I was emerging from the bushes carrying a sizeable shipment of turtle eggs packed in Styrofoam boxes and loading them furtively into the aircraft parked on a little-used highway, it occurred to me that our actions could easily have been misinterpreted, especially as our flight would take us over northern Mexico and into Texas at low altitude. After all, many individuals in the area derived some or all of their income from similar kinds of activity....

"We had been advised to land on the highway at Padre Island to minimise the overland journey for the eggs. They told us to circle the Ranger Station three times and they would then stop the traffic for our landing. This we did, but it was a public holiday and it was also lunchtime. We circled three, four, five, seven, ten times, but no-one emerged from the Ranger Station to attend to our urgent need. Kim looked up and down the highway at the holiday traffic, and we realised that landing would not be easy. Finally we saw that there were some short, dirt roads, relatively free of traffic, running perpendicular to the main road. We selected one of these for the landing and stopped just short of the intersection with the main highway."

They were immediately surrounded by hundreds of concerned Texan holidaymakers, who thought the plane had made an emergency landing. Fortunately, the ridley conservation program had been well publicized by the National Park Service in the local media and when they explained that they were carrying turtle eggs there was instant recognition. They then spent some time signing autographs and having their photographs taken. The two thousand eggs were installed at the hatching facility after the staff returned from lunch.

(A current staff-member comments: "To this day, communication during the 'getting eggs out of Mexico' stage continues to be a problem, because arrangements often have to be changed at the last minute. Usually the NPS is on standby for several days, not knowing exactly when the eggs will arrive.")

In 1981, Pat Burchfield succeeded Peter Pritchard as head of the U.S. contingent at Rancho Nuevo, and has continued up to the present time. Ms. Bower was succeeded after three years by Buddy Mattix, who also donated his flying time and the use of his plane to the project.

A nesting turtle at Rancho Nuevo approaches its reception committee.

XI Nesting At Rancho Nuevo

WHEN THE MOTHER of one of the year's head start groups emerged from the sea in May, there was a reception committee waiting. Two of the Mexican-American field crew were taking shelter from the sun in a grass-roofed shelter and an armed Mexican Marine stood nearby, ready to protect turtles and eggs from human or animal predators. Some Mexican schoolchildren and their teacher chatted with him as they waited hopefully to see a turtle nesting.

Sharon Manzella, a young career biologist from the National Marine Fisheries Service in Galveston, was resting in the shade of a motorized beach trike. She became quite excited when she saw the grey shape crawling over the wet sand, because this was the first nesting turtle she had seen and it was the last of her ten days at Rancho Nuevo. She had hoped to become involved in an arribada. Now she would like at least to be able to take photographs of a nesting turtle to show to her colleagues at NMFS and to the nearly six thousand schoolchildren and others who visit the Galveston laboratory each year.

The turtle crawled up the beach, using first her right foreflipper roughly in unison with her left hindflipper, and then the other pair of opposite flippers, pausing to rest from time to time. The brisk wind swept a dusting of sand over her tracks and lowered the air temperature so that she did not heat up too quickly. Later it would help to disperse odors from her nest that otherwise might attract predators. While she was moving up the beach she repeatedly pushed her snout into the sand as though testing it. Perhaps the taste or smell of the sand confirmed that she had returned to the place she left as a hatchling, or perhaps she was merely testing the warmth and dampness of the sand to determine when she was far enough

Biologist on a beach bike takes a bag of eggs to the hatchery building.

above high tide level to begin excavating her nest. She crawled straight ahead until she reached a point halfway up the first line of dunes, then stopped, and worked with her flippers and the edges of her shell until she had excavated a shallow pit for her body. Sharon readily saw the point of this — the temperature of the surface layer of sand was about 120°F, much too hot for bare feet.

A hopeful black vulture had flown up un-noticed and would feature in Sharon's slide collection, sitting on one of the 8-foot posts that stand at intervals along the beach. The numbered posts were intended to be used as reference points by the roving patrollers who inspected the twenty-mile nesting area several times a day and radioed the locations of nests to their colleagues on egg recovery bike patrol.

Ignoring the watching people, the turtle, now with eyes closed, buried her lower jaw in the sand, working her head from side to side and digging her foreflippers firmly into the sand for stability. Then she began to dig the nest cavity with her hindflippers, curling them alternately into the sand and flicking it into a neat pile about 6 feet in front of her.

As the hole deepened, she gradually raised the front of her body so she could stretch her hindflippers further into the sand. When the depth had reached about 20 inches and the back of her carapace had sunken a little into the hole, she splayed out her hindflippers and began to lay her eggs. With eyes glazed, she lifted her head, opened her mouth a little and sighed profoundly as each new lot of eggs slipped from her body.

During this process she was unaware that a marine biologist from the FWS team was lying on the sand behind her. During the pauses in her excavations the biologist had dug a small access hole into her larger one. Now she was catching the soft, white, ping-pong ball-sized eggs in a sterile plastic bag. The eggs were kept out of contact with the sand so they could not absorb anything from the beach that might later cause the turtles inside to return there to nest.

After laying 110 eggs in twelve minutes, and oblivious to the fact that they had all been intercepted, the turtle began to fill the nest with sand, using a circular motion of her hind flippers. Then she performed the 'ridley rhumba', rocking from side to side as she vigorously thumped her shell on the sand over the nest to compact it, and when that was done to her satisfaction she began to turn herself around in a circle, flipping sand in all directions with her front flippers. Finally, after casually throwing a few flipperfuls of sand backwards with alternate pairs of flippers, she made a turn to the left, ready to head back to sea.

Before she could leave, a student from Tampico's Universidad del Noreste and Al Barr, a biology teacher from Houston, measured her carapace (about 26 inches long and 24 inches wide), and clipped a numbered metal tag onto her left foreflipper. When she returned to nest again, perhaps once or twice more before the season ended, or in later years, the tag would identify her for records of nesting dates, times of day, locations and numbers of eggs in each clutch. The tag might also be reported by a fisherman who accidentally caught or killed her in a net, or by somebody who found her washed up, sick, injured or dead, on a beach.

When the biologists had finished with her, she began to move heavily back across the sand, wearied by the nesting and the heat. By the time she reached the sea again she had been out of the water for about fifty minutes.

Sharon was to hear later that 609 turtles were recorded nesting between April and July. Seven nested three times, 52 twice, and the rest just once, for a total of 675 nests.

HUEVEROS

"For the most part the egg thieves, or hueveros (pronounced wayveros), are cowboys who work in the area and they ride onto the beach with their horses and dogs. They're in and out, really, before we have an opportunity to either catch or observe them," Pat Burchfield says.

"For a huevero to be arrested there has to be a Marine, a fisheries biologist, and a Pesca inspector on hand. It is a complicated process that on occasion has resulted in the arrest of hueveros at the sanctuary. During one season, the same man was apprehended and sent to jail twice, and on the second occasion they confiscated his burro, which represented a fairly major economic loss to this individual. Once word of this had gotten around there was considerably less egg-stealing activity on the beach."

Says Woody, "The only way to be sure of protecting a nest early in the season, before the Marines arrrive, is to sit on it. They take any that you don't sit on. The cowboy circles round you on his horse, smiling, with his big silver spurs dangling, and he has four or five big dogs with him. You smile back at him, but you don't feel very secure sitting there on the ground in a pair of cut-off shorts."

"One elderly man was a regular offender. Whenever we came into camp he seemed to be sitting there in the shade, trussed up by the Marines, with his burro grazing nearby."

Problems with hueveros are more likely to involve turtles nesting singly, especially before the Marines arrive, and it is estimated that nowadays fewer than twenty nests are taken in a season.

Each year the 2,000 Operation Head Start eggs are collected without having touched the sand. The remaining 50,000 to 80,000 eggs laid during the season are dug up and transplanted to man-made nests in two well-guarded beach corrals. The eggs have to be transplanted within a few hours of laying because moving them after this time might kill the embryos. Nearly two months later, while the head start hatchlings are slogging their way over the sand at Padre Island, the beach-corral hatchlings are being released near the waterline at Rancho Nuevo.

The intention is to leave no nests in place on the beach, for even with constant guard and prompt collection, coyotes, coatis, skunks, feral dogs or ghost crabs are likely to plunder a nest. Given the opportunity, a coyote will creep up behind a nesting turtle and steal the eggs while they are being laid. In contrast to the situation where large numbers of turtles nest at once and 'predator swamping' ensures that some nests are left unscathed, isolated nests are subjected to tremendous pressure from predators. René Márquez and some Mexican students conducted an experiment in which they protected several nests at the places where the turtles had left them and watched at night to check for predator attacks and identify the predators. They found that, on average, each nest was subjected to no fewer than seven predator attacks during the course of one night. It is for this reason that one of the major priorities of the Mexican/ American crew is to move every nest it can find into a protected corral. And, as noted above, the field workers also have to contend with local poachers, the 'hueveros', who are very prompt to empty nests if the guards arrive after the nesting season has begun.

A biologist lies behind the nesting turtle, collecting eggs in a plastic bag.

International team members measure and tag the nesting turtle.

RECORRIDOS

Nobody can predict when the turtles will arrive. Typically four beach patrols, or recorridos, are made each day on the three-wheeled motor cycles, beginning at 6 a.m. When a turtle is seen, the essential job of the patrol is first to avoid disturbing it before it actually begins laying eggs, and then to tag and measure the turtle, and finally to mark the location of the nest for collection.

Nests are collected as soon as possible after laying. If it is a solitary turtle on a quiet day, all of the biological data surrounding the nesting activity are noted. On most days during the four-month nesting season only a few turtles, or none at all, are seen nesting — sometimes there will be no turtles on the beach for a period of ten or eleven days. Other times are busy with around 20 to 50 arriving on the same day, and on two or three random days each season a small arribada of 80 to 150 turtles will come ashore to lay their eggs. When this happens, the beach workers are hard-pressed because nobody can rest that night until all of the eggs have been moved into corrals.

The appearance of an arribada seems to be triggered by gale-force winds off the Gulf of Mexico. At the height of an arribada there might be fifteen people, working in different rows, simultaneously digging facsimile nests in the corral, all using post-hole diggers to get down about eighteen inches and then using a scallop-shell, a plastic spoon, or a hand to produce the flask-shaped bottom.

If there are hueveros on the beach during an arribada, the practice is to mark the nest with some kind of code and place the marker stick several meters away from the nest, or place it on an oblique angle, or otherwise try to confuse the egg thieves. However, usually there are no hueveros on the beach on arribada days because of the Marines and the large number of biologists and students working on the team.

XII Life At The Turtle Camp

MEANWHILE THE HEAD START EGGS have been taken over the dunes by beach trike to the turtle camp. Here the international team of biologists stays for five months, its only contacts with the outside world being sporadic visitors and a radio powered by a car-battery. The camp is organized and run by the Mexican government, assisted by Brownsville's Gladys Porter Zoo and others acting on behalf of the United States Fish and Wildlife Service. Qualified observers agree that, by and large, the Rancho Nuevo project is very well run, which surely represents an astonishing achievement in view of the number of different government and non-government agencies involved in both countries.

There is a camp cook (provided by Mexico) who cooks for the Mexican crew, the U.S. crew, the Mexican Marine contingent and any visiting students. Living accommodations for the two crews are shared but conditions are still fairly primitive. Mexican government employees usually sleep in the block building; Mexican students sleep in tents. The original tents for the U.S. crew were recently replaced by a solid barracks building, so that field workers and equipment are no longer liable to remain sodden for weeks at a time during the hurricane season. There are now gasoline and diesel-powered generators, but the latter only operate for one hour a day, so temperatures in the egg hatchery building must be controlled by opening and closing doors, covering windows, or wetting the floor to provide cooling by evaporation. Because the Rancho Nuevo project has been regarded as a showcase for the Instituto Nacional de la Pesca, quite a lot of money has been spent since the early days on basic amenities such as concrete buildings to house Mexican equipment and personnel.

WHERE DO MARINE BIOLOGISTS COME FROM?

Both teams use the Ranch Nuevo project as a means of training people to work in biology and on other turtle projects. A new group of Mexican students from the Universidad del Noreste at Tampico arrives every week or two to help the field crew, and the U.S. crew normally includes, in addition to graduate students, several undergraduate students majoring in biology. A significant proportion of these are likely to go on to do graduate work.

Many people who are now making their careers as professional marine biologists or conservationists have gained valuable experience and unforgettable experiences as field workers at Rancho Nuevo. A partial list of alumni from the U.S. crew includes Woody, Pritchard and Burchfield, Rod Mast (Species Conservation Program, World Wildlife Fund International), Dr. Mary Mendonça (Postdoctoral Fellow in Zoology, University of Texas), Tim Clabaugh (Head of the Environmental Services Division, Seminole County Government, Florida), Carol Woody (Fisheries Biologist with the U.S. Forest Service in Alaska) and Laura Tangley (Assistant Editor for Bioscience magazine in Washington, D.C.). Lynn Corliss and Carlos Hasbun have worked on turtle projects in several countries, and Georgita Ruiz, now at the University of Veracruz, has headed two turtle projects in Mexico. Angie McGehee is completing a Ph.D. in Marine Science at the University of Puerto Rico, and Richard Byles, who tracked sea turtles in Chesapeake Bay for his Ph.D. dissertation, is now working with Woody as the Sea Turtle Biologist with the Endangered Species Office, Fish and Wildlife Service, Albuquerque.

Inside the hatchery building, Pat Burchfield, U.S. Field Group Coordinator and General Curator-Herpetologist of the Gladys Porter Zoo, supervises the care of the Operation Head Start eggs. He is an intense, dedicated person in his early forties, of medium height and strongly built, with curly, greying hair and a cheerful, open face. He does this work in addition to his regular job at the Zoo.

Burchfield has continued Pritchard's work of measuring temperatures and humidities in natural, man-made and Styrofoam box nests at different times during incubation, and he knows the most favorable combination of temperature, humidity, and type of handling that will help the eggs develop into healthy hatchlings. It is now known, for example, that it is dangerous to the embryos to transport the eggs during the first two weeks of incubation because, unlike the situation in a chicken egg where the embryo floats near the middle, in a turtle egg at the same stage the embryo migrates to the top, where it becomes attached by some delicate membranes that can easily be ruptured by movement. This probably accounts for the low incubation yields obtained by Adams and his coworkers when the eggs were taken overland to Padre Island. However, there are other factors to consider.

Even if the turtles nest when expected, he has difficulty deciding when to collect the eggs. The best time to export them without causing injury is two to three weeks after they are laid, so he has to try to predict when the export documents will be issued. In some years, when the documents arrived late, the eggs initially prepared for export had to be kept at

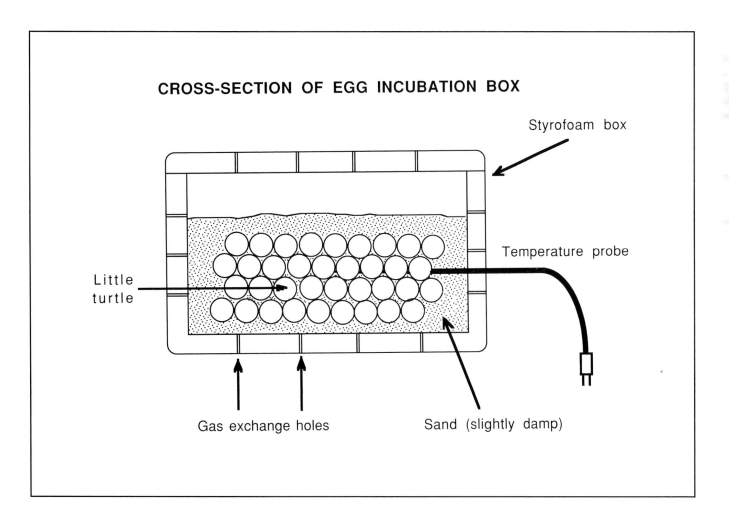

CROSS-SECTION OF EGG INCUBATION BOX

Styrofoam box

Temperature probe

Little turtle

Gas exchange holes

Sand (slightly damp)

Rancho Nuevo for hatching and release and a second lot collected for Padre Island. Ideally, the head start eggs should be gathered while only a few turtles are nesting, so as not to interfere with the main work of the sanctuary, which is the tagging of nesting turtles and removal of clutches of eggs to the protected corrals.

A worker wearing sterile surgical gloves transfers the clutch of eggs, complete with the viscous laying fluids around it, onto one inch of carefully chosen, sifted and moistened Padre Island sand in a box made of insulating polystyrene foam. The role of the laying fluid in the wild is possibly to protect the eggs from dehydration during the early stages of incubation, which is also a desirable feature in the Styrofoam box. The eggs are layered on top of each other so that they touch and will be able to share the heat produced during the last of three phases of incubation. More sand is gently poured down the sides and another one-inch layer is spread on top, to ensure that the eggs will be exposed only to Padre Island sand and will not touch the sides of the box. The eggs' temperature will be monitored regularly with a probe and can be raised or lowered by replacing or removing the lid of the box and by warming or cooling the surrounding air.

After several weeks, when the 2,000 eggs have been collected, Burchfield again faces the problem of exporting them to the United States. As usual it is complicated by a range of factors which include the unpredictable arrival of the turtles, the weather, the tide, the requirements of the border-crossing, and Matamoros Airport being closed at night because there are no landing lights.

Field worker passes an egg box to Buddy Mattix beside the Cessna on the beach at Rancho Nuevo.

XIII Flying Turtle Eggs

IN THREE PREVIOUS YEARS the Rancho Nuevo runway has been under water. This year it is dry but remains very rough, even after a truck has devoted several hours to the traditional procedure of smoothing out cattle tracks and ruts by hauling around a large beam weighted with field workers. The Cessna's pilot, Buddy Mattix, who has flown turtle eggs through thunderstorms and landed in highly adverse conditions to comply with time limits on export permits, now makes a critical inspection of the airstrip and decides to take off from the beach. Twenty boxes containing the twenty clutches of eggs are loaded into the Cessna aircraft, each box labelled and equipped with its temperature probe and a record of the clutch's history, and it is time to leave.

The takeoff, effected at low tide, is uneventful. Their first landing is at Matamoros, on the Mexican side of the Mexico-U.S.A. border, where Burchfield presents border officials with permits from various Mexican government agencies, from the United States Fish and Wildlife Service, and from the Convention on International Trade in Endangered Species of Wild Fauna and Flora. A Mexican fisheries inspector is on hand to receive the guia de pesca,[12] a form executed earlier with Mexican officials at the turtle camp. This permit at State Department (Secretaria de Relaciones Exteriores) level, good for 72 hours, says that the eggs are a gift from Mexico to the United States, and is necessary for the legal export of the eggs. The Mexican consul in Brownsville, on the other side of the border, has been sent copies of all the papers and is prepared to assist if problems arise. Finally, crew and cargo are minutely inspected by officials of the United States Customs Service. On this occasion it appears that everything is in order and they can take off again right away.

In 1982 the aircraft and eggs were confiscated by Mexican Customs at Matamoros because of a new regulation that the Mexican Customs Service had introduced without advising the affected government departments in either Mexico or the United States. The U.S. State Department

Cessna prepares to land on the road at Padre Island.

and Fish and Wildlife Service, their Mexican equivalents, and Pesca were all left equally in the dark. Gladys Porter Zoo personnel shuttled to and from Matamoros Airport, an hour and a half drive each way, two or three times a day for three days, opening and closing aircraft doors and Styrofoam box lids and adjusting shields of reflective foil in the plane's windows. Outside the plane the temperature rose to 100°F while Zoo and Fish and Wildlife officials worked feverishly through successively higher echelons of government. Finally the signature of an official in the Mexican President's Cabinet was obtained and the eggs could be released to go to Padre Island. In the end, only the normal proportion of eggs failed to hatch, so the frantic efforts to keep the unborn turtles from becoming hard-boiled must have been successful.[13]

Pat Burchfield notes, "One helpful customs officer in Matamoros offered to keep the eggs in his refrigerator. When we informed him that this would kill them just as surely as overheating, it caused a bit of a row."

A few minutes after takeoff, Mattix, Burchfield and the turtles are flying over Padre Island, a long, narrow, almost barren sandbar that stretches along the coast of Texas from Brownsville to Corpus Christi. Their destination is the Padre Island National Seashore, which occupies about 70 miles of beach and dune land in the middle of the island. In this zone all wildlife is protected by the National Park Service, which takes responsibility for the care of all turtles while they are in the park.

A road-block has been set up near the north end of the park. Two lines of resigned motorists watch and wait as the plane lands on the road and Park Rangers and biologists load the boxes on the back of a pickup truck for the short ride to the turtle shed. At the turtle shed, hidden around behind the ranger station, it is found that the top layer of sand in the boxes has become very dry so some distilled water is sprinkled onto it, on Burchfield's advice, simulating a rain-shower. An extra layer of sand and a plastic-coated screen are added to the top of each box before it is placed inside a second Styrofoam box, for better insulation, and hoisted onto one of three tiers of shelves. The temperature probes from the egg boxes, from three boxes containing sand alone to serve as controls[14], and from three probes measuring air temperature at each shelf height, are connected to a thermograph that records the temperatures in the boxes and in the shed at hourly intervals. During the last 20 days of incubation the temperatures of boxes containing eggs should be higher than the temperatures of the controls. When this is so, the biologists know that the clutches are alive and generating their own body heat.

EGG DELIVERY UPDATE

In l988, Burchfield decided to move the eggs as quickly as possible from the rudimentary incubation hut at Rancho Nuevo to the better equipped one at Padre Island. The transfer would take place before the first rise in egg temperature, due to metabolic heating, that was normally used as an indication that the eggs were viable, so he sent the zoo's assistant curator of reptiles, Colette Hairston, to Rancho Nuevo to "candle" some eggs from each box. She darkened the room, held the eggs against a light so that she could see through the parchment-like shells, and was able to report that all of the boxes appeared to have live embryos developing.

Then the necessary portfolio of permits arrived from Mexico City and, on June 15th, Burchfield and his unnamed pilot, headed south from Matamoros in a twin-engined Piper Aztec that would take them to Rancho Nuevo in an hour. However, the rainy season in Mexico was well under way and about half-way to Rancho Nuevo they entered a blinding rainstorm. Twenty minutes later, when they emerged above the Mexican fishing village of La Pesca, they saw that the area had been inundated and there was standing water everywhere.

" We knew Rancho Nuevo would be the same," says Burchfield. "Sure enough, the dirt airstrip was under water and the camp looked like a lake, with the trucks all parked above the high water mark. The tide was too high to land on the beach, so we flew south to Barra del Tordo. Same story — everything under water. Then we flew low to look at the highway that Peter Pritchard and Gray Bower had used some years earlier — brand new telephone poles and lines! No chance there either, so we headed back to La Pesca, with the idea of landing and waiting for low tide. Another rain-storm prevented us from even finding La Pesca, let alone the unlit airstrip. No ridley eggs today!

"Back at Brownsville I called Donna Shaver at Padre Island and said we would try again in five days. It rained for the rest of the week, but this time we planned to arrive at the camp later in the day, at low tide, so we could land on the beach."

On the second trip, made with Vicente Mongrell, his second-in-command in the Rancho Nuevo project, the plane's engines refused to turn over at Brownsville and the pilot had to call on the services of a mechanic with a battery charger. Not a good omen.

"We alighted at Matamoros and filed a flight plan for Rancho Nuevo and Barra del Tordo. We did not particularly want to land anywhere that was not on our flight plan because we might be mistaken for contrabandistas (smugglers) and detained by the Mexican Army or Marines."

Box continued

At Rancho Nuevo, the turtle camp and landing strip were under water as anticipated, and the pilot made a couple of low passes over the beach before deciding to land in the space between two large driftwood logs. He had to brake hard to avoid the second log, which had the effect of burying the plane's nose gear deep in the sand. So, while Burchfield and Mexican officials attended to the guia de pesca, the field team dug out the plane and then carried the egg boxes from the truck, one by one, across a rivulet that had appeared in the sand bar.

"When we tried to start the engine we found the battery was totally dead again," says Burchfield. "Richard Byles put a four-wheel drive truck in front of the nose and fitted jumper cables by removing a small panel between one propeller and the wing. He clambered up into the cabin and started the engines. Then, ever so skillfully, he slid down like an eel between the roaring prop and the edge of the wing. He removed the jumper cables, which were carefully lifted up out of the way by a beach worker sitting on top of the nose, and replaced the battery panel with his screwdriver within inches of the roaring prop. Then, from where I was standing on the wing above him, I gave him a hand up out of his precarious situation."

"Once aboard, we lumbered and lurched forward in the soft sand, bogged down, and got stuck again. Hmmm. With props still roaring because we were afraid to turn them off, we tied a rope to the nose strut and dragged the plane about. Then we attached the rope to the tail and began to drag it down the beach to the firmer sand, right next to the surf, with the truck straining all the way against the pull of the propellers. Finally we were right against one of the logs that marked the end of the runway, and they could let us go.

"The beach was rough and the plane bumped and hopped along, gradually picking up speed. When the landing gear hit soft patches in the sand the plane slowed and strained dramatically, so the pilot gave it full throttle. It felt as though we were just about to lift off when a wave hit our left wheel and shoved the plane to the right. Suddenly, a spray of water washed over the plane and I thought we had crashed into the surf. Then the water cleared from the windshield and I realized we were airborne. I breathed a sigh of relief, sat back in my seat, and noticed a strange odor. It was the smell of burning electrical wiring! The pilot opened some vents to let the fumes out while I watched for signs of an imminent emergency landing. He continued to climb and I thought he was gaining height ready to glide, in case the engines quit, but after what seemed an eternity, with the fumes coming and going, he finally spoke up and said he was flying on to Brownsville."

"I could see the flames behind the instrument panel and watched the gauges melting," Vicente Mongrell told Burchfield later, after they had landed.

Box continued

It was late and the airport was closed. They called the control tower and waited for a customs official to come and clear the shipment of eggs.

"Our pilot told us that the plane had had it," Burchfield says, "and suggested we could either truck the eggs to Corpus Christi or drive him to Harlingen International Airport to get another of his planes. Worrying that the eggs might become chilled, we reluctantly opted for the latter. At Harlingen we pulled a single-engined Piper Cherokee from its hanger, removed one seat and quickly loaded the egg boxes.

"Then he asked if either of us had a flashlight so he could read his gauges. Fortunately Vicente did have one, and we did eventually take off. When the lights of Corpus Christi came into view, after an hour's flight, the pressure of weeks of anticipation and the day's harrowing events suddenly abated and life was good. In the distance I could see Donna Shaver and the group from the National Park Service anxiously awaiting our arrival. We had made it!"

[Donna Shaver reports that these eggs had a 91.6 percent hatch rate, the best at the park to date.]

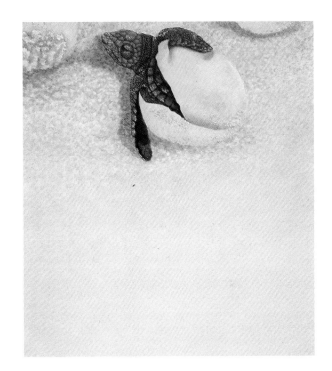

Hatchling emerges from egg.

XIV   Hatching At Padre Island

NATIONAL PARK SERVICE Turtle Biologist Donna Shaver has nursed successive crops of eggs through hatching and imprinting for the past seven years. Her serious demeanor reflects the responsibility of ensuring that incubation and hatching of the precious eggs goes smoothly. She sleeps on a stretcher in the air-conditioned part of the turtle house, waking at intervals to check temperatures in the incubation area. The room she sleeps in is actually a laboratory, occupied mainly by work-benches and scientific instruments, and its walls are papered with temperature charts and conservation posters.

The incubation area is roofed but open to the outside air, with wire-mesh walls covered with plastic to conserve heat, and shade screens that can be pulled down to prevent overheating by the intense summer sun. There is an electric floor heater for extra heating and a fan for cooling.

When the air around the boxes becomes too warm she lifts the box lids for a few hours to allow them to cool. The aim is to keep clutch temperatures between 86 and 90°F during the middle third of incubation, so as to produce more females than males — temperatures just below 86°F have the opposite effect. (Incubation temperature determines the sex of the embryo in many reptiles, including sea turtles.) Box lids are usually removed from 6 a.m. to 9 a.m. to match the lower temperatures in natural sea-turtle nests at that time of day.

At the beginning of July, almost two months after the start of incubation, signs of imminent hatching begin to appear. When hatching time is near, incubation temperatures rise, and once this has happened the surface layer of sand is checked every morning. Sometimes sunken circular areas appear on the surface as sand fills the space previously occupied by the yolk sacs that nourished the little turtles in their eggs. Sometimes a faint tapping sound, like a fingernail touching a desk, can be heard as the first tiny turtles begin cutting a way out of their shells and moving around. It usually takes from a few hours to two days for the turtles to emerge from their shells, absorb the parachute-like yolk-sacs half as long as themselves, and begin to struggle towards the surface.

A hatchling is held above its incubation box.

Donna Shaver comments: "A few clutches each year hatch after a circular area of sand begins to sink, with the turtles emerging from their shells and becoming active in a few hours to two days. These turtles appear on the sand surface in the state we term 'juvenile frenzy'. Usually, however, we detect hatching by noticing a few individuals in the top layer of eggs pipping their shells. It then takes about one to two days for them to crawl out of the shells, finish absorbing their yolk sacs, and be ready for transfer. At transfer, some may be buried down in the sand a bit, so we must dig down to free them. When this happens, few of the transferred hatchlings are active. Most individuals absorb their yolk sacs before leaving the shell and hence before reaching the surface of the sand — normally turtles do not become active until the yolk-sac is absorbed."

The one we shall call Little Turtle is busy in the middle of the clutch, slicing her shell with the sharp, raised bump, misleadingly called an egg tooth, that a newly-hatched turtle has on the tip of its snout. A few hours later the mass of tiny, dark-grey turtles are weakly struggling over one another, Little Turtle among them. As they flipper upwards through the sand their eyes are kept closed, or barely open, to protect them from the sand grains.

During the morning check a few turtles are found on the surface of the sand. Donna puts on sterile gloves before handling them, so as not to confuse the imprinting process, and moves them to their own transfer box, keeping them separate from the hatchlings of other clutches. Then Donna digs down gently and removes the rest of the new hatchlings before they can become trapped and suffocated in the sand, which is becoming saturated with egg fluid.

The remaining eggs in the clutch are covered again with the mesh and surface layer of sand to retain heat are and allowed to incubate for an extra two days to make sure that they are not going to hatch.

The turtles are held in the transfer boxes for about a day to gain strength and develop their infantile frenzy. In this hyperactive state, which lasts two or three days, they have the energy to hurry over the sand and swim far out to sea beyond the breakers. Now, confined in the boxes, they are climbing over one another, waving their flippers with a vigorous swimming action and becoming more and more agitated.

This is the start of a busy period for the workers. Because the eggs were collected over a period of three weeks at Rancho Nuevo, it will take about three weeks for all of them to hatch, and the hatching and the release and retrieval phases of the project will be going on at the same time. The separate hatchings will be set loose on the beach for their crawl to the sea on fifteen July mornings, spread over three weeks, and on each occasion somebody will have to make the return trip to deliver them to Galveston.

Imprinting on the beach at Padre Island. Donna Shaver releases some hatchlings.

It is 8 a.m. on a fine, breezy morning. Park Service biologists and rangers drive a pickup truck loaded with four priceless boxes of hatchlings over the rutted dune track to Closed Beach. One of the first things they will have to do on arrival is reprimand some riders in a dune buggy, who have ignored signs saying that the beach is closed to traffic, and send them back to the road. Riding on the back of the pickup are five high school students from the Youth Conservation Corps (YCC). Supervised by Jenny Bjork, a biologist who co-ordinates the Park's endangered species and oil and gas monitoring research, and other resource protection projects, the students sweep and shovel seaweed and lumps of tar from a seventy-foot long stretch of shore along the high tide line, fill in crab holes in the dry sand above high tide, and scrape a crowd-control marker on the beach at one side of the cleared area.

Wearing sterile plastic gloves, Donna and seasonal park ranger Kirsten Brennan place five rows of ten hatchlings at two separate points about a hundred feet from the sea. A mixed crowd of twenty adults and children, who have just arrived with a ranger conducting a nature-study walk, stand watching behind the line on the sand, or enter the release area one or two at a time to take photographs. Later some will help guard the turtles while they cross the sand, or help recapture them from the sea. A television film crew and sundry writers are also present.

The hatchlings set off down the beach, giving the impression of taking their bearing from the sun shining low over the ocean. In case this is really what they are doing, the watchers take care not to cast shadows that might confuse them. Some of the hatchlings travel quickly and reach the sea in about fifteen minutes; others have to be warmed for a while by the sun before they will get under way, and some even need to be placed on their backs briefly and then righted, to mimic the rough and tumble of a natural emergence from the nest, before they begin to move. The slowest takes more than an hour to reach the water. One confused hatchling

Little Turtle crawls over the sand.

flippers around in circles and has to be picked up from time to time, air-lifted a few feet, and restarted in the right direction. This one would probably not have made it in the wild.

The helpers keep moving their eyes from the sky to the sand and back again, on the lookout for hungry seagulls and sand-colored ghost crabs, counting and recounting the hatchlings, and alert for the flick of a claw from a crabhole. Whenever a new crab-hole appears it is covered with sand and stomped shut. The squadron of hatchlings begins to fan out as they approach the water, and at this stage they have to be watched very carefully in case they stray too far from their anticipated path and get trodden underfoot. No turtles have been lost on the beach during ten years of imprinting.

Jenny Bjork says: "This was the first time I had participated in a hatchling release. I began working at Padre Island National Seashore nine months ago. After participating in the head start turtle release in March, and monitoring nesting loggerhead turtles in the Florida Keys, my anticipation was high. My first priority was the protection of the hatch-lings. Since Donna was a pro at imprinting turtles, my next priority was to be available to media personnel and visitors.

"The little hatchlings reminded me of wind-up toys once they started their frenzied crawls. Their enormous front flippers moving alter-nately in rapid succession made me want to laugh... After a period of rapid crawling for several seconds, the hatchlings need a rest. At this stage they strain their necks, raising their heads to orient themselves. Then the little ones seem to do a series of pushups and it's off to the races again. Moist sand at the wave edges stops them for a moment, then they seem to realise that this is where they are supposed to go. The first wave usually sends them tumbling. After they have done that a few times, they expertly dive under the wave and with those large flippers are fast, power-ful swimmers."

Little Turtle plowed over the sand so fast that she almost caught up to the slowest turtles from the previous batch. She was quite hard to see as she moved over the beach because her back was covered with san-dand she was only about the size of a book of matches. When a lump of sand blocked her way she stopped using her foreflippers alternately and dug them both into the sand together to heave herself over it. Once, in her enthusiasm, she lost her balance and flipped onto her back, where she lay for a few seconds, kicking and rocking, until Donna's plastic-gloved hand turned her over. She seemed determined enough to have righted herself, eventually.

Just as her mother had done on her way up the beach at Rancho Nuevo, Little Turtle pushed her snout into the sand as if tasting or testing it while she was flippering along. When sand grains got in her eyes she paused and brushed them away with a flipper. Towards the end of her journey she crawled across a sign reading: THE SEA, with an arrow giving the direction, that some helpful person had scraped on the sand. Near the water's edge the surface was damp and smooth and she could go even faster. Then the first wave washed the sand from her back and once again she was black and hard to distinguish from a small blob of tar. She was drawn out by a wave, then washed back, and drawn out again by the following one. As soon as it was deep enough she began to paddle vigorously and was soon clear of the wave zone. A television cameraman, attracted by her outstanding athletic prowess, kicked off his shoes and entered the water, joining a line of people with nets, to record Little Turtle's first taste of the ocean.

Luckily for her, this brief freedom was about to end. Estimates vary, but it is likely that not more than about one hatchling in a hundred survives to adulthood if set free at this stage. In the first year, many become items on a menu for organisms farther up the food chain. Forty helpers, each holding a white, aquarium dip net, stood up to their knees in the water, waiting to scoop up Little Turtle and the others.

Helpers dip hatchlings from the sea.

The turtle scoopers kept their eyes firmly fixed on the small turtles that were passed on to them by the on-shore traffic controllers. Newly hatched turtles are already expert swimmers and could easily dart past and disappear under a wave. Little Turtle found herself being caught up in a white net and lifted out into the sunlight again. A plastic-coated hand placed her gently on a layer of moistened rubber foam in a box and one by one her brothers and sisters joined her. The lid was replaced after each addition to protect them from the ninety-degree heat.

Jenny Bjork adds: "A nine- or ten-year-old boy in the ranger's party was watching very intently. When I went over his mother told me he had given his entire allowance to the HEART organization to save ridley sea turtles. I took his hand and we joined the nearest line of volunteers netting turtles in the water. I put a net in each of his hands and stood behind him with another, just in case. I explained that he should let the turtle swim into the net, then gently raise it out of the water, and cover the net with his hand. A ranger would come to him, give him an empty net and take the net with the turtle. We had to wait for several minutes before a turtle entered the water near us. He did an excellent job of netting the turtle, then brought the net to his face and examined the little guy with glee. His smile, interest, caring and satisfaction will never be forgotten."

Only four groups of fifty turtles were released that morning and they had all been recaptured by 11 a.m., before it became too hot for them to continue to be active. When all of the turtles had been accounted for, the workers piled onto the truck with the boxes and headed back along the dune track to the laboratory.

Now it was time for vital statistics. Little Turtle's shell was 1.6 inches long, she weighed half an ounce, and she was adjudged a prime specimen of a Texican turtle with no external deformities. The information was entered in her records. It was too soon to tell that she was female.

Early that afternoon, she and the others were placed in a tub on foam rubber saturated with sea water. Four tubs from the day's imprinting, along with their information sheets, were loaded into the back of a car that was air-conditioned just sufficiently to keep the temperature at about 85°F during the five-hour drive to Galveston. A slightly weary YCC volunteer and a blond-haired seasonal ranger named Elizabeth Cheeseman drove away with them.

The care given to the eggs ensured a better chance of hatching and survival than in the wild, and only 235 of the original 2,011 had failed to hatch, a yield of 88.3 percent. The biologists stored the failed embryos in preserving fluid. In the weeks ahead they would determine their sex by examination of internal organs (gonads), and try to determine the time and cause of death.

*Thousands of hatchlings inside
'corralitos' as an arribada hatches.*

XV Meanwhile Back At The Rancho

AFTER DELIVERING THE head start consignment, Pat Burchfield flew back to the turtle camp at Rancho Nuevo, where many of the year's crop of more than 50,000 hatchlings were still waiting to complete their incubation and be released. Also, the camp was shortly due to be visited by up to three hundred Mexican schoolchildren, plus their teachers and parents, from Rancho Nuevo, Barra del Tordo and the surrounding districts. These visits were begun as a public relations exercise to dispel various misconceptions among the village people about the beach activities, including a dark suspicion that the camp had actually been set up to enable all of the eggs to be taken to America, where they would obviously fetch a much higher price. They became annual events because of their evident value as a means of teaching the local community about turtles and about conservation. This year there would be two visits on two separate days.

The official invitations to the children from camp administrator Manuel Sánchez did not specify a date — that would be up to the turtles. A visit would be scheduled when it appeared that there would be a sufficient number of hatchlings, at least hundreds and preferably thousands, to make it interesting and exciting for the children. The time of hatching could usually be predicted to within a few days from the date when the eggs were laid, with allowance for the warmth of the season, and more precisely from the appearance of a depression in the sand above the eggs. As Burchfield explained on a tape:

"Anywhere from a few hours to a few days prior to seeing hatchlings on the surface there is a cavity or concavity in the surface sand. This is created by the baby turtles inside the eggs having absorbed their yolk material during development. Once they have slit the eggs and commenced moving, sand will filter down to take up the void created by the loss of yolk material from the entire clutch of eggs.

"Usually the turtle corrals are checked all night long for hatchlings because, as with most species of sea turtle, the majority of them will hatch under cover of darkness. This is one of their survival adaptations. Normally only the nests that naturally hatch very late or during the morning are retained for release by the children — we do not stockpile turtles for this function!

"The biologists try to release the turtles as close to their natural hatching time as possible, bearing in mind that when a nest hatches a biologist has to count the live turtles and open any unhatched eggs to record at what stage of development the baby turtle died if it didn't hatch — or was the egg perhaps infertile? Once this is done, the hatchlings are taken from the corral in a bucket or a Styrofoam box and released at different sites along the beach, allowing the baby turtles, or crias as they're called in Mexico, to crawl across the sand and into the water, while carefully supervising to avoid predation by ghost crabs or other predators. The hatchlings are released onto the beach at different sites because this helps to avoid predators becoming conditioned to come to the same place every morning to eat baby turtles.

"We try to time the visits of school children to coincide with the emergence of a large number of nests. Once we have seen the depressions in the sand, it usually doesn't take more than a day or two to work out the logistics with the local teachers and so get them to the camp."

The Turtle Fiesta

Visitors from Rancho Nuevo began to arrive at the camp very early in the morning, the little girls in bright dresses and the boys in their best jeans and T-shirts. Biologists and technicians distributed crayons (provided by HEART, of which we shall hear more later) and turtle conservation coloring books[15] (provided by the National Marine Fisheries Service), and the visitors were subjected to educational talks and demonstrations by biologists, interspersed with fun and games that included sack races, footraces, consumption of soft drinks, and a feast of watermelon. About two weeks later there would be a follow-up visit to each classroom by a biologist from the turtle camp, to determine how much the children had learned.

For all of the visitors the major event of the day was the opportunity to see, usually for the first time, not merely a live turtle but hundreds of live baby turtles at close range, and to help release them into the sea.

"The children are very much fascinated by the small turtles," Burchfield says. "The only time they've seen a sea turtle, in most instances, was after it had already been killed and brought ashore in a net. Or perhaps, in some cases, they had seen eggs that their father had brought home to sell at the market in Tampico. Virtually none of them had seen a baby sea turtle, or any live sea turtle for that matter, before coming to the turtle camp."

Because the eggs from a medium-sized arribada had been hatching, the biologists had worked through the night. At dawn, as a mist was rising from the ocean into the cool, damp air, the work intensified. Hatchlings from seventy-one of the hundred and fourteen arribada nests were on the surface and in a frenzied state before the sky showed the first pink tinge of sunrise.

"Once the first turtle has erupted from the sand, almost all the other hatchlings from a nest are usually on the surface and very active within thirty minutes, though sometimes they take an hour, and occasionally, two," says Burchfield.

"When they pip the shell there is probably some inter-egg sensitivity — maybe the scratching — that triggers them to emerge at the same time, so that it's a group effort to get to the surface. However, the turtles which are less developed for one reason or another remain in the egg for more hours or days to absorb their yolk sacs. In the wild their chances of survival would be slimmer, because coyotes and other predators are attracted by the nest odors. The stragglers probably wouldn't make it, but I don't know that for sure. Some might survive...

"Judging from their very active crawling state, most of the hatchlings would have entered the water before sunrise if they had hatched naturally. The advantage to a small, grey-black, hatchling turtle of crossing a pebble and shell-strewn beach under cover of darkness is obvious when you start thinking about predators."

The first release was made soon after children began to arrive on the beach. A bucket of hatchlings that had been collected just before sunrise by biologist Daniel Rios was gently poured out onto the sand. The children first helped him place them by hand on the beach a few meters above the water line, then watched with delight as they scrambled energetically over and around one another in their haste to get to the sea. With so many watchers about there was no need to guard the turtles against gulls or ghost crabs but, although the nearby waves appeared innocent, nobody could guess how many sharks or redfish were waiting a little way out for some small turtles to join them at breakfast.

Releases continued until mid-morning, when the last brave company of hatchlings was sent on its way. By then the sun was quite high and the little turtles sometimes became confused and wandered in circles. The children did not mind having to pick them up and set them back on the right path, but it was a good time to stop. Soon it would have been too hazardous for the hatchlings, because they could not control their body temperature to withstand the increasing heat. The children returned to the picnic and the sack races, and then it was time for siesta.

Rancho Nuevo children and adults enjoy fiesta after releasing hatchlings.

WHERE DO HATCHLINGS GO?

In the previous year, twenty-four hatchlings marked with brightly colored spots were released before dawn and then followed out to sea by two biologists with scuba gear and others in a Zodiac inflatable boat.

"On several occasions our swimmers in the water or we in the boat would inadvertently come too close to a hatchling, whereupon it would stop swimming, remaining motionless to avoid being seen," says Burchfield. "Once we had retreated two metres or so they would recommence swimming as though nothing had happened."

The hatchlings were marked with brightly colored spots that had been attached with an adhesive made by mixing five packs of gelatin in one cup of water. The spots were previously tested on Ila Loetscher's turtles to make sure they would fall off after one day. Radio transmitters attached by Velcro harnesses had already been tried in the Galveston laboratory and not recommended, because their weight affected the turtles' behavior and ability to swim and breathe, and the harnesses restricted carapace growth. The biologists had been worried that the spots might draw the attention of predators but, on the contrary, gulls flying over the hatchlings seemed to be confused and deterred by the colored spots. They invariably flew on their way after having taken a good look at the strange and unappetising little turtles.

The divers found that the marked hatchlings, like their unmarked siblings, swam due east into the Gulf after they had cleared the breakers. After one-and-three-quarter hours, at one-and-three-quarter kilometers offshore, the divers lost contact with all but five of the marked hatchlings, but could still see several unidentified hatchlings in the distance, all heading due east. The hatchlings were now swimming at a depth of two to three meters and remaining submerged for up to two minutes.

"At this point we had difficulty in spotting the turtles, due to the reflection of the rising sun," Burchfield says, "so we decided to follow a single hatchling for as long as possible. At two hours and two kilometers off shore, hatchling number three was still swimming actively due east at the same depth of two to three meters."

Afraid that they might encounter a strong current, the biologists paddled shorewards. (Their Zodiac had no outboard motor, to avoid the risk of disturbing the turtles or hitting them with the propeller.) They planned to follow a larger number of hatchlings for twelve hours in the next season, using two Zodiacs and a parent vessel, but abnormal extremes of temperature delayed hatching into August and the attempt had to be postponed a year because they were too busy with the new releases.

Hatchlings being put into their buckets for
head starting at the Galveston laboratory.

XVI The Head Start Class

AT THE NMFS LABORATORY in Galveston a small team of biologists — Tim Fontaine and Ted Williams among them — had been busy preparing a nursery for Little Turtle and her head start classmates.

Tim, a career biologist in his forties, would like to be more involved in basic research, but he finds that turtle husbandry, in what he likes to call the turtle barn, takes too much of his time. He is described by a good friend as a large teddy-bear of a man, with brown hair and beard and an enormous sense of humor. In his spare time he writes poetry and country-western ballads. Ted, a few years younger than Tim, wears glasses, is wiry and soft-spoken, and is the person people turn to for help when some piece of equipment cannot be made to work. A very hard worker himself, he lives right at the laboratory, in a house-trailer parked next door to the turtles.

The workers had filled fifteen long, narrow, fibreglass tanks with sea-water and were making daily checks of the salt content of the water and of the air and water temperatures. Heaters were already installed in readiness for the cooler weather to come.

Suspended in each narrow tank were 108 yellow plastic buckets, all provided with holes in the bottom so that water could pass through. Each turtle would have its own bucket because hatchling turtles, like the young of many species, do not get along well together and are likely to fight over food. This lesson was learned the hard way in the first year of Operation Head Start, when the little turtles were kept together in small groups and they bit one another incessantly. The biting led to injury, disease and sometimes even death. One day the biologists noticed that the number of turtles recovering from injury or illness in individual buckets was greater than the number remaining in groups, and it was decided that they should all be given private quarters in future.

Dr. Charles Caillouet, Chief of the laboratory's Life Studies Division, was telling a small visitor about the hatchlings while Elizabeth Cheeseman and Ted placed them in their buckets. Caillouet, of medium height, with dark hair and moustache, is both a perfectionist in his work and dedicated to turtles, and has the sense of humor that is needed to manage the combination. He moved from shrimp to turtle research at a time before turtles were in the public eye. Now, thanks in part to the success of his work, the turtle field is an attractive one for young biologists. He is also the artistic creator of a strikingly realistic ridley turtle marionette, which he designed for HEART to sell as part of its effort to raise funds for turtle conservation.

The newly arrived hatchlings were quite perky and soon began to explore the confines of their buckets. For less active new arrivals, Ted would keep the water level low at first so that they could rest on the bottom and recover from the long drive.

The dark shape of Little Turtle lay sprawled on the bottom of her bucket for several minutes, until she recovered from the journey and began to paddle around. For the next ten days she continued to live on the nourishment from her egg sac. Then, after that was used up, she nibbled at the floating pellets of special turtle chow that were sprinkled in her bucket twice daily, and before long she began to look forward to feeding time. She was weighed at intervals and her chow ration was steadily increased as she grew heavier. Her bucket stayed clean because uneaten food and wastes fell through the holes into the main channel. Her attendants replaced the seawater in the tank with a fresh supply three times a week and scrubbed the inside surface of the tank once a week — this is one way that biologists pay their dues after they join the turtle community.

Among the people looking after Little Turtle was biologist Kathy Indelicato (née Williams), a placid person in her twenties who is noted for her affection for turtles and for the calming effect she has on them. One day Kathy noticed that the pellets were floating around, uneaten, on top of the water in the yellow bucket and Little Turtle herself was drifting about listlessly, obviously unwell.

A sick bay had been established by placing three rows of larger blue basins on raised shelves at the middle of one of the two plastic–covered greenhouses where the turtles lived. Kathy picked Little Turtle up gently and deposited her in a blue basin. The problem was soon diagnosed as a bacterial infection, and Kathy injected an antibiotic into her shoulder muscle and gave her extra attention, changing the water around her more frequently. After a few days, Little Turtle seemed better and was moved back to her bucket.

"Some people we've had working with us cause the turtles to become very agitated, just by their presence, whereas other people don't upset them at all," Tim Fontaine says. "Kathy has a phenomenal effect on them. When she picks them up for weighing they become very still and docile. Her younger sister Jo, who joined the staff recently, shares her touch. Most of the biologists who have worked with sea turtles for me, even the men, develop a very protective, motherly instinct towards the turtles, sometimes even overly protective — Kathy once nursed a turtle in her bathtub at home all weekend because it needed intensive care. We even have to be careful about the colors we wear in the turtle house," Tim adds. "Turtles are quite sensitive to color and may become agitated when they see bright colors, especially red. Once an empty basin somehow got a spot of red paint in it. Later, when it was put back into use, the turtle pecked the paint spot quite aggressively."

HEAD STARTING

"The head starting portion of the program is extremely important because we continue to have a very high incidental take of the adult and juvenile turtles in the Gulf of Mexico by both the U.S. and Mexican shrimp fleets," said Pat Burchfield, late in 1987. "I feel that, until trawling efficiency devices are required and installed on both the Mexican and U.S. shrimp fleets, we should head start more hatchlings — both those imprinted at Padre Island and others imprinted at Rancho Nuevo. The latter have also been head started at Galveston in the past.

"In recent years Larry Ogren, of the NMFS in Florida, has been observing larger numbers of juvenile Kemp's ridleys in Florida waters and in other northern Gulf of Mexico and Atlantic areas where they once abounded. So something is working — it could be the head starting at Galveston, the increased production of hatchlings at Rancho Nuevo, or more likely, a combination of both."

It is interesting to try to calculate how the number of head start yearlings compares with the number of yearlings produced from the hatchlings liberated at Rancho Nuevo, when estimated survival rates are taken into account. Nearly 14,000 healthy, documented, Operation Head Start yearlings have been released into the Gulf over the last ten years. (This is in addition to several hundred that have been moved to marine aquaria to form the basis of a captive brood stock.) The best current estimate of time to maturity for Kemp's ridleys in the wild is

Box continued

about ten years, with an uncertainty of at least two or three years either way. For the hatchlings incubated in corrals at Rancho Nuevo, if we take the commonly-held view that about one in a hundred survives to adulthood and assume a constant mortality rate, we find a 63 percent probability that a hatchling will survive its first year. This figure is certainly too high — the first year is acknowledged to be especially vulnerable. If we make the arbitrary assumption that 90 percent of the mortality before adulthood actually occurs in the first year, the number of survivors from the 50,000 released each season at Rancho Nuevo works out to be 5,000. This would give a total of 50,000 yearlings produced over ten years, or about four times the Galveston total. If, instead, only 70 percent mortality is assumed in the first year, the number of Rancho Nuevo yearlings works out to 150,000 over ten years, or about ten times the head start total. However, as Larry Ogren and others have pointed out, there is no scientific basis for the figure of one percent survival to adulthood of Rancho Nuevo hatchlings, which at best has the status of a rough 'guesstimate'. It is also true that, because of their sedentary upbringing, head started turtles are likely to be handicapped, at least initially, by a lack of stamina in comparison with their wild counterparts, although this can be countered by the observation that they are less likely to have been debilitated by disease, pollution, and the continual struggle to stay alive.

Larry Ogren, Fishery Research Biologist at the NMFS Panama City Laboratory in Florida and a long-time collaborator of Archie Carr's, is of medium height, solidly-built, and youthful-looking, with fair, thinning hair and a complexion that hardly ever tans. As a scientist he is inclined to be practical rather than academic, and he has the combination of a sense of humor and great dedication that seems to be a requirement for work in this field. One of his main interests is the ecology and migrations of sea turtles. Ogren comments:

"While sightings and captures of adult ridleys at sea have become rare events, there is now an apparent abundance of 'yearlings' and slightly older, foot-long, juveniles and subadults being observed and captured in coastal areas of the Gulf. The yearlings are about 8 inches in carapace length when we first find them and have just shifted from the pelagic stage (feeding on the surface) to the benthic stage (feeding on the sea floor). The abundance of subadults is also reflected in the number of strandings recorded over the past few years. However, the ones we have found so far were all wild turtles and so must represent the Rancho Nuevo hatchlings, not the Padre Island ones.

"Since 1978 we have tagged 352 wild turtles and all but one were juveniles. Of these, 221 were found on the south-east Atlantic coast, mostly at Cape Canaveral, and the other 131 were in the northern Gulf, mostly the Florida Gulf Coast."

Tag returns from live head started turtles, reported by Jim McVey and Charles Caillouet, indicate that they adapt well to conditions in the wild. The recaptured turtles doubled, tripled or even quadrupled their weight in two years after their release. They were reported from Mexico, all the Gulf coast states and

Box continued

up the east coast to New York, and three travelled thousands of miles from their release site, reaching France and Morocco.

Sharon Manzella's files at the NMFS Galveston Laboratory show that 547 head started turtles had been recovered from the 1978 to 1986 year-classes by the end of 1987. Nearly 60 percent were alive and were returned to the sea, occasionally after rehabilitation. Most were reported from Texas (360), Louisiana (67) and Florida (49), with fewer coming from Mississippi (6), Alabama (4), Georgia (10), South Carolina (12) and North Carolina (19). Virginia, Maryland, New Jersey and New York reported two each. Seven reached Mexico, two were found in France and one in Morocco. For two the location was unrecorded.

Thus the tag returns reported by McVey and Caillouet suggest that head starting is working, and the abundance of young, untagged turtles reported by Ogren indicate that the Rancho Nuevo effort is working. There remains the minor mystery of why head started turtles have not so far been found among Ogren's sample of the juvenile population. The answer possibly lies in the differences in the ages of the turtles when they enter the system of ocean currents, and in the places where they enter, whether off Rancho Nuevo or Padre Island.

Of course it must be added that both the head starting and Rancho Nuevo efforts become futile if the turtles die in shrimp trawls before they reach breeding age.

School class, teacher and Janie Lowe examine Little Turtle.

XVII The Class Visit

IN SEPTEMBER, when school resumed after the summer vacation, biologist Jo Williams began to take bookings for the three thousand pupils who would visit the laboratory during the year. The first teacher who phoned was Karen Mozara from Galveston's Central School, who wanted to bring her science club students to see the hatchlings before they were two months old, while they were still very small.

The same pupils had visited the year before, when she taught them at Weis Middle School. At that time they had become so eager to help the turtles that they had formed a HEART (Help Endangered Animals — Ridley Turtles) Council under her sponsorship, and persuaded the whole school to become involved. In the end, all twenty of the home rooms had sponsored turtles in addition to ones sponsored by the science club.

Now aged 11 and 12, the pupils gathered around and admired the perfection of Little Turtle as she sat calmly on Jo's hand, puzzled by the strange shapes and noises around her. They all marvelled that so much time and effort had been spent in bringing her to Galveston. Beside them stood fair-haired Janie Lowe, illustrator of this book, who had flown down from Lubbock to join the class visit.

They also saw the slides that Sharon Manzella had taken at Rancho Nuevo. They saw the desolate, shrub-covered dunes, the primitive buildings, the outdoor showers, the armed guard, and the hopeful vulture. She told them how hot and tiring it had been patrolling the beach, with temperatures often in the nineties. There were many different views of Little Turtle's mother nesting and then returning to the sea.

"What a pretty color she is underneath! All creamy."

"She doesn't look very comfortable, over on her back like that."

"Why is she lying on her back in that one? Did she fall over?"

"She must have put her foot in a crab-hole."

Biologist Jo holds an amputee hawksbill in the turtle hospital.

"The reason she's upside down is that my film ran out."

"YOU turned her over?"

"It was the only way I could get her to wait while I changed it."

They couldn't leave without visiting their old friend Bolivar in the turtle hospital, where larger sick or injured turtles live in large tanks until they can be released after rehabilitation. Bolivar, a young hawksbill, was first found five miles east of the Bolivar Ferry landing at the entrance to Galveston Bay, stranded and tangled in sargassum weed. Six days after being released from hospital, Bolivar was rescued again from the same shore. Biologists concluded that the turtle might have suffered brain damage when first stranded on the beach in the hot sun. Bolivar remains confused, but swims around happily in permanent custody in the psychiatric tank. On the other hand, Bolivar might be perfectly aware of what he or she is doing. (The biologists do not know yet whether Bolivar is male or female.)

Jo carefully lifted up Bob, a small hawksbill whose right foreflipper had been amputated before the turtle was a year old. A plastic onion sack was wrapped tightly around it when Bob was found on the beach. Now the turtle just bobs up and down in the tank, and eventually will live at the Sea-Arama Marineworld. Denton, a class-of-1985 ridley, had been discovered on the beach with a cracked carapace, possibly caused by a boat propeller. The Houston Zoo applied a fibreglass patch to act as a splint, after which the back healed well. The patch had since been removed and Denton was due to be released soon. There was still a dent on the turtle's head, which accounted for the name.

Captain Hook, a wild two-year-old Kemp's ridley about a foot across, was caught by a man fishing off a pier with a hook and line. Dr. Joseph Flanagan, the Houston Zoo's veterinarian, removed the 3-inch hook and the captain was recovering well. Another wild ridley named "Oiliver" had been found on the beach at Galveston Island, heavily coated with oil both internally and externally. Oiliver needed a two-year stay in the hospital.

Traveller, a head-started turtle, had been severely wounded, perhaps by a shark attack, when he was found stranded on the Bolivar Peninsula beach, fifteen days after his release off Padre Island. HEART chose these same children to organize a turtle-naming contest for him, giving the winner a sea turtle T-shirt.

Some Kemp's ridleys that had been hatched at the turtle farm on Grand Cayman Island were isolated in quarantine during the class visit. They were being fed and cared for in the same way as the Padre Island turtles.

Children adopting turtles have red hearts pinned to the wall.

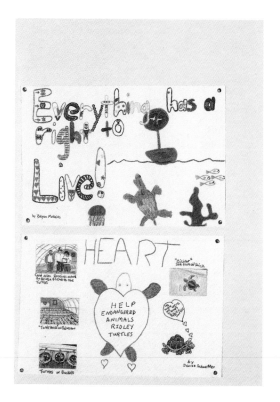

Children's Kemp's ridley conservation posters.

Four pupils had saved their pocket money so they could adopt and name a sea turtle of their own. Jo was ready to write the names, together with the name of the school, on red plastic hearts and pin them to the wall in the turtle house alongside countless others.

"Let's give them Spanish names, because the eggs were laid in Mexico," said Tina. It was easier than she realised. She and Joe called their turtles Tina and José. "When we go swimming at Galveston next spring, we'll be able to think of Tina and José turtle swimming somewhere in the Gulf of Mexico with us", said Joe. Janie and Tim decided to call theirs Juanita and Timoteo. They could only guess at the sexes of the baby turtles and, because females far outnumbered males in the head start class, it is really an extraordinary coincidence that they happened to guess correctly.

During their visit the class looked at sea turtle conservation posters drawn by other pupils who had visited the laboratory. The posters were displayed on the walls of the turtle buildings and biologists' offices. Some were the finalists of a poster competition organized by HEART.

After they all left, Little Turtle continued to swim around in her bucket, neither knowing nor caring that her name was now Tina.

HEART (Help Endangered Animals — Ridley Turtles)

The thousands of school pupils and other members of the non-profit HEART organization come from schools (elementary through high), scout groups, herpetological societies, conservation organisations and science clubs in every state throughout the United States, from Maine to Florida and Alaska to Hawaii. HEART also has members in Mexico, Canada, England, The Netherlands, Venezuela, Japan, Australia and New Zealand, and *The Heart-break Turtle* , a videotape has been sent on request to Pakistan and the Philippines. About half of the HEART members live in Texas. They have formed eighty HEART councils, each with an adult sponsor. Sometimes whole schools are involved, raising as much as $1000 each in a year.

Sponsoring or 'adopting' a turtle through HEART costs $4. This pays for the turtle's special chow for its ten-month stay in Galveston. HEART members and supporters have provided all of the turtles' food for Operation Head Start since 1982.

Visitors inspecting the HEART Hotel.

XVIII A Fine Day At The Turtle House

IN FEBRUARY, when the turtles were six months old, newspapers announced that the Kemp's ridley sea turtle head start operation would have its annual open house from 9 a.m. to 3 p.m. on St. Valentine's Day, February 14th, during Galveston's Sea Turtle Week. Hundreds of people from Texas and beyond drove to Galveston and followed the heart-shaped signs to the NMFS facilities on Avenue U. (At present the open house is held on some weekend in the first half of February, and Sea Turtle Day replaces Sea Turtle Week.)

Early in the morning a table piled with turtle souvenirs was set up in the street outside the laboratory gate. Mrs. Carole Allen, founder and chairperson of HEART, and several of her helpers had been hard at work since Christmas, getting ready for this day. Part of the cost of each souvenir would sponsor a turtle, so many red hearts were waiting to be filled in and pinned on the walls inside.

Soon visitors began to arrive. Most, not knowing what to expect, were surprised and intrigued by the hundreds of yellow buckets, each with its small black tenant. Tina stared back at them, wondering about the objects that clicked and flashed in her direction. Now she half-filled the bucket and was really quite photogenic. As she had grown larger a narrow, cream-colored edging had appeared around her flippers, head and carapace.

The new architecturally-designed, 800-bucket, HEART Hotel was open for inspection. HEART and its contributors had helped plan the hotel and paid for a large part of its construction. New contributors were promised a turtle house-warming, a limited edition HEART Hotel T-shirt, honorary "share-holder" status, and inclusion of their names on a commemorative plaque. Long-time HEART supporter and Mayor of Galveston, Jan Coggeshall, officiated at the dedication and ribbon cutting ceremony. The ribbon, with a big bow, was attached to the back of one of the six-month-old residents of the hotel.

HEART table,outside Galveston laboratory.

A shrimp net equipped with a TED (turtle excluder device) designed by NMFS was on display between the other two turtle houses. Visitors examined the grating that had been sewn into the net to stop turtles from drifting to the cod-end of the net as it was towed through the water. They also saw the hole in the top of the net just in front of the grating, through which turtles could escape, and the gaps in the netting on each side of the TED, where unwanted finfish could escape by swimming forward. Shrimp could not escape in the same way because they would not be able to swim against the current, and would be carried through the grating into the back of the trawl.

Visitors lingered in the turtle houses, asking the biologists questions about the turtles, HEART, and the displays on the walls. Younger members of HEART stood at key points to direct them to the turtle hospital and to a slide show telling the turtles' life story. Afterwards most returned to the turtle houses to admire the turtles again before leaving. People kept saying, "Aren't they cute!" to nobody in particular.

"My most touching memories are of children seeing sea turtles for the first time, and of letters containing a nickel or maybe a row of pennies wrapped in crumpled paper and mailed to me to help the sea turtles," says Carole Allen. "Sometimes a child sends his entire allowance. And once, after an open day on Valentine's Day, I found a row of little hearts pinned where only the turtles could see them, above the buckets in a corner of the turtle house that not many people visited."

SUPER HEAD STARTING

The optimum size or age at which head started turtles can survive in the wild is not yet known, according to Dr. Edward Klima. For this reason, "super head starting" or "extended head starting" is being tried. Super head starts, that are released into the environment as older animals, come from the laboratory's ordinary head start classes and from captive stock distributed among aquariums in the United States.

A hundred members of the 1986 head start class were kept at the laboratory instead of being released with their classmates and were tagged with the passive integrated transponder (PIT) in March, 1988. Two months later, fifty of these two-year-olds were released along with the 1987 year class and 130 turtles that had been head started at Galveston after hatching from eggs laid at the Cayman Turtle Farm in the British West Indies. (The parents of the last group were head start turtles from Galveston.) The remaining fifty, two of which had a temporary stay at the San Antonio Zoo because of front-flipper bone problems, were kept at Galveston for a third year.

Fifty members of each year class will continue to be kept at the laboratory so that fifty three-year-old, extended head started turtles can be released annually with the yearlings of the current class.

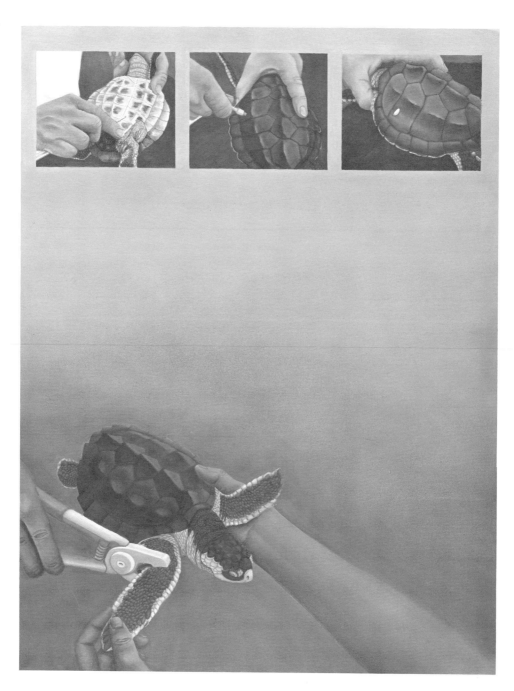

Tina receives living and metal tags.

XIX Tagging And Release

THE TURTLES ALL HAD TO BE TAGGED before release so that they could be recognized and reported wherever they were found. This is the most reliable way for biologists to gather information about their growth, physical condition, and migrations. Also, if the turtles returned to nest at Padre Island, the tags would be the only means of identifying them as head start turtles. Tagging is not as easy as it sounds, because external metal tags fall off after about three years, internal magnetic tags need special equipment (X-rays or magnetometers) to detect their presence, and living tags are difficult to recognize as tags, let alone decipher, by anyone not involved in the turtle project. All three tagging methods were employed in the hope that at least one would remain useful over the whole of the turtles' lives. Tagged head start turtles from previous years had been reported from as far north as New York and as far east as France and Morocco.

Tina's living tag had been applied by plastic surgery when she was fourteen weeks old. A small core from her off-white plastron (or breastplate) had been transplanted to the hole left by a similar core taken from her dark grey carapace (the shell covering her back). The location of this contrasting spot of living tissue was different for each year's head start class, so it amounted to a code for the year, one that would maintain its identity over the years because it would grow at the same rate as the rest of her carapace. Now a small metal tag stamped with a code number and return address was clipped to the edge of Tina's right foreflipper. Next, a tiny magnetic pellet, slightly smaller than a grain of rice, was injected into her left foreflipper where its detection would be a matter of moderately high technology. When tested, Tina's flipper produced a satisfactory reading on the magnetometer scale.

This year, Tina and her classmates were also subject to an experimental, high-technology tagging procedure, in which a device called a passive integrated transponder (PIT for short) was inserted under the skin of her shoulder. The PIT was a small, cylindrical object that resembled a half-inch length of pencil lead. When stimulated by a hand-held sensor aimed at Tina's shoulder, the PIT responded by broadcasting a letter code which was received and displayed in a window on the sensor. With the aid of the code, a technician could associate an individual turtle with a detailed record going right back to the tag number that her mother had been assigned on the beach at Rancho Nuevo. By the time all of the class had been multiply tagged, release day was very close.

Radio transmitters are sometimes attached to a few of the turtles to track their movements for four or five weeks, until the batteries fail, but that was not done with Tina's class. Flipper-printing is also being tried. This is similar to taking a person's finger-print and is done in the hope of being able to identify the turtle later from flipper-print images stored as computer records, once the records are sufficiently extensive to provide a useful database.

By May, Tina was the size of a small salad plate,[16] weighed two pounds, and almost filled her bucket. It was time for her to be released into the Gulf of Mexico. Late one evening she was moved onto the traditional bed of foam rubber soaked with seawater, this time inside a large cardboard box. A total of one thousand members of her class were placed in similar boxes, each box holding eight turtles in two layers of four, and the boxes were carried out and stacked on the decks of three trucks.

Tina stuck her head out through the hole at the corner of the box and was confronted by a wall of faces poking through similar holes in other boxes. Behind her, on the same level of the box, her three companions for the journey were José, Juanita and Timoteo, the other turtles adopted by Karen's pupils. At this age they were less aggressive than before, but the biologists still thought it advisable to pack them with their heads pointing away from one another, towards the corners of the box. After a short interval the trucks moved off and drove through the night, arriving at Port Aransas soon after sunrise.

At Port Aransas, the turtles that had their heads sticking out of the holes watched with interest as NMFS personnel formed a line to hand the boxes from the trucks onto the University of Texas research vessel "Longhorn". When all were aboard, the sturdy vessel motored out until it was well away from the shore and the biologists began to release the turtles, one at a time, lifting them from their boxes and setting them down in the water at intervals of about twenty feet. The biologists tried to choose areas free of flotsam and patches of sargassum weed in an effort to reduce the liklihood of the turtles coming into contact with floating balls of tar.

NMFS biologist Tim Fontaine drops Tina from the boat.

Tina was among the first to be dropped into the water by Tim Fontaine. When all of the classmates had been released into the Gulf, the vessel motored back to Port Aransas, and an important phase of the turtles' life was past.

From the turtles' point of view it had all been rather straightforward and effortless. Now read on...

"The NMFS staff suffer far more than the turtles at release time," says biologist Dickie Revera with conviction. Dickie, a slim, warm person with glasses, greying hair and a vibrant personality, has been working in the laboratory since 1974 and with turtles since 1980. She has participated in every aspect of the program and makes it obvious that she cares deeply about individual turtles, really resenting it when things don't go right for them. She tends to mother the younger members of the team.

"One year I was very disappointed because I couldn't go down with them," she adds, "but I didn't mind so much when I heard what a wretched time they'd had. Some of the kids on the release were super-fit, but they came back absolute rags."

Release day begins at midnight, when the staff get together to place wax-coated cardboard boxes on planks next to the yellow buckets, line them with foam rubber, and hose the foam until it is soaked through, ready to receive the turtles. Packing a thousand active two-pound turtles into boxes, with eight turtles to a box in two layers, can be a trying operation. The turtles usually become rambunctious and want to get out, so the boxes have to be taped shut.

It is about 3 a.m. by the time the staff have finished loading the boxes onto the trucks. Then, because the light in the turtle houses is not very good, a final check is made with flashlights to ensure that none of the turtles has been left behind. For most of the workers this is a good time to change out of wet clothing and sit down with a restoring cup of coffee, while listening to the unique sound made by a thousand sets of flippers scratching vigorously against the sides of a hundred and twenty-five cardboard boxes. Usually Carole Allen is there to help with the graduating class and has brought cookies. When the coffee and cookies are gone, it is time to set off for Port Aransas, which is located on the northern tip of Mustang Island, just north of Padre Island.

"One year we blew a radiator hose at 3.30 a.m. and clouds of steam billowed from the engine so we couldn't see the road," Dickie remarks. "Tim had wisely spread the load over three trucks, just in case of an emergency. Joe Flanagan, the vet from the Houston Zoo, who had helped us load up, now helped to unload our forty-two boxes of turtles and stack them on top of the boxes in the other two trucks, before he went to work for the day. We left the empty truck by the side of the road with a note on the windshield."

At Port Aransas there is barely time for the biologists to have a bite of breakfast before they load the turtles onto the boat. (Normally they are too busy at sea to have lunch.) They form into a line and hand the hundred and twenty-five boxes, each weighing about twenty pounds with its lively contents, from the trucks to the deck of the "Longhorn". The boat leaves the dock at about 7.30 a.m. with a complement that includes biologists, turtles, television cameramen and reporters.

It can take up to three hours to reach the release area, depending on the state of the sea and the weather. Then, for the next five hours, it is slow speed ahead and plenty of action on deck as the turtles are lifted from their boxes and dropped one by one into the sea.

"We arrive back at the dock about five," says Dickie. "Only after we've hosed down the boat and taken the boxes to the dump do we get time to photograph the dirty, hungry, and sometimes seasick release crew and head wearily for the nearest motel. There are very few photos of the actual release that have been taken by NMFS staff!"

Tim Fontaine adds, "Normally it's rough at sea at that time of year, but in 1983 it was particularly rough. We had several TV crews with us on the Coast Guard cutter "Point Baker", together with newspaper reporters and visitors. Everybody was seasick except for me, one of my workers Bill Browning, and Van Hackett from Channel 13, Houston. Bill and I released the turtles and Van covered it for the news media. We were gone for about seven hours and were very glad to get back, I can tell you!"

Underwater photographers and a U.S. Navy reporter-photographer were among the media people recording the off-shore release in 1986. In 1985 the Houston Chronicle covered the event from the very beginning, when the turtles were being put into the boxes. In the laboratory report for that year is a (flippant?) note reading:

"We were especially pleased that the ridley release was covered by media representatives surnamed Rizley (Galveston Daily News) and Rigley (KTRK-TV, Channel 13)."

"It's very quiet and empty back at the turtle house after the last release of the season," Carole admits. "We're relieved the job is done, but there's definitely a letdown. You realize that usually there's a lot of noise from all the flippers scratching against the sides of the buckets and from the water being splashed around. It's a bit depressing, and you feel like a mother hen. You're glad they're free but you're worried about them because you know what's out there. You're wondering how they're doing."

Tina "in flight" in the sea.

XX Freedom

TINA'S WORLD HAD SUDDENLY EXPANDED. Once clear of the boat, she swam in circles at first, temporarily forgetting that she was no longer confined to a bucket. Then, excited by her newfound freedom, she swam away swiftly in a straight line, not caring where she was heading. Her oar-like foreflippers cut powerfully through the water while her hindflippers trailed behind, steering her streamlined body like twin rudders.

She was truly in flight through the water. Her foreflippers rose and fell in unison, slowly and gracefully like the wings of a large bird. Occasionally she glided to the surface and lifted her head into the air for a few seconds to take a breath and look around before slowly descending again.

Tina was now almost as big as the cormorants and hawks and most of the predatory fish that would have taken her in one gulp when she was a hatchling, and she was no longer afraid of them. She knew instinctively to watch for and hide from the menacing shapes of sharks and barracudas that could bite off a flipper or slice a piece out of her shell. A large shark might even swallow her whole.

She could not withdraw her head and flippers inside her shell for protection as a tortoise does. Sea turtles have abandoned that passive defense in favor of strong swimming muscles and a streamlined shape. Now she must either outdistance her enemies or hide from them. If she needed to hide, it would help that she was camouflaged like a military aircraft — light on the bottom and dark on top — so that large fish looking up from below would find it hard to see her cream plastron against the light surface of the water, while birds looking from above would have difficulty distinguishing her dark carapace from the deep water.

After swimming for a time, Tina began to tire from the unaccustomed exercise. For a while she floated effortlessly amongst a raft of sargassum weed that was drifting along in the current and had somehow

Tina floats on sargassum weed in the current.

111

escaped contamination by tar and floating trash. When she looked more closely, she found that the weed was alive with crabs, worms and other small animals that would become favorite snacks. They were all camouflaged to match the weed. For a while she rested, contemplating a small crab.

Ten months of growth had changed her shape, as well as the color of her plastron and skin. Her carapace was almost as wide as it was long, and her head and flippers were smaller in proportion than when she was a hatchling. Intricate dark designs enhanced the cream skin on the lower side of her head, neck and flippers. Her plastron was plain cream, unlike those of some of her classmates, which sported dramatic black markings. In time she would lose her distinctive colors and take on the drab coloration of the sea-bed in the shallows.

When her energy had returned she ate the crab and found that she liked the taste, then took a mouthful of sargassum weed and sea water, expertly squirting excess water out through her nostrils. The hooks on her foreflippers made first-class implements for pulling superfluous weed away from her mouth. It seemed a pleasant place to stay, and a pleasant way of life, so she remained there for a while, eating the small denizens of the weed and steadily growing larger.

After she had spent some months living amongst the sargassum, the diet composed entirely of small snacks began to pall and one day she slipped below the weed to explore farther afield, nibbling on a passing jellyfish as she went. This time she headed shorewards, towards the shallow bays of the Gulf coast. She would find the shallows full of delicious blue crabs. Juanita was there already, eating her fill.

XXI Our Heroine Is Almost Swallowed Alive

TURTLES ARE NOT ALONE in regarding the shallow waters of the Gulf as an excellent source of food. One day, while she was browsing along the bottom in a particularly fertile patch of sea-grass, Tina suddenly became aware that a huge green fish was swooping up behind her with its mouth agape. She could not escape by moving to the side out of its way so she tried desperately to outswim it, but it was travelling much faster than she could, and soon the enormous mouth extended from the sea floor to far above her. It did not, of course, belong to an ordinary ocean predator, but to a shrimp trawl that was being towed by a boat some distance ahead.

Tina drifted back into the opening amid a cloud of shrimp and small fishes, while the shrimp boat moved inexorably onwards. It appeared certain that she was doomed and all her fighting instincts were aroused, but there was nothing for her to struggle against. And then, where the net grew narrower, her carapace collided against some metal bars with a solid clunk, and the bars steered her upwards and out to freedom through a trapdoor in the top of the net. Shaken and disturbed, she headed out into the deeper waters of the Gulf and did not return to the shallows for several days — not until her memory of the experience had faded to the point where it was less potent than her appetite for crabs.

It was fortunate that Tina had encountered a shrimp boat whose owner was cooperating in NOAA (National Oceanic and Atmospheric Administration) tests comparing a TED-equipped trawl with a standard one, and that she had been in the path of the TED-equipped trawl. If she had been in the path of the standard trawl she would not have escaped.

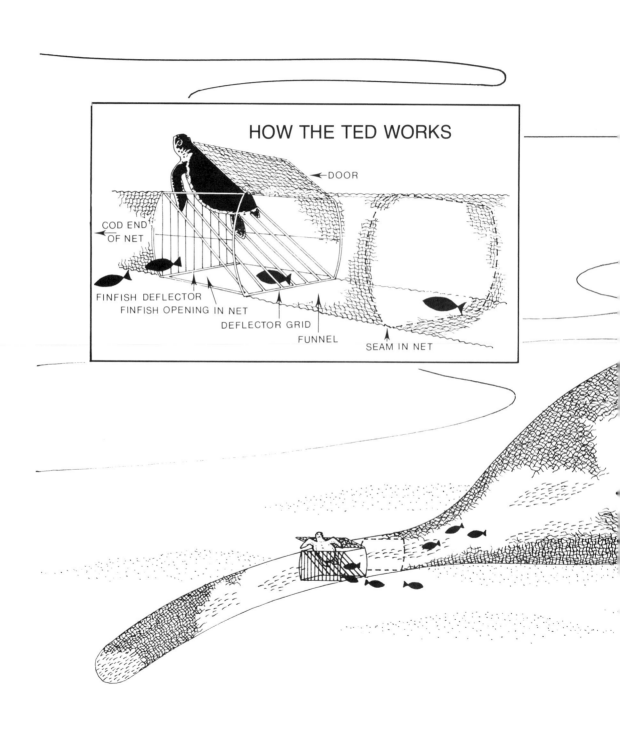

HOW THE TED WORKS

DOOR

COD END OF NET

FINFISH DEFLECTOR

FINFISH OPENING IN NET

DEFLECTOR GRID

FUNNEL

SEAM IN NET

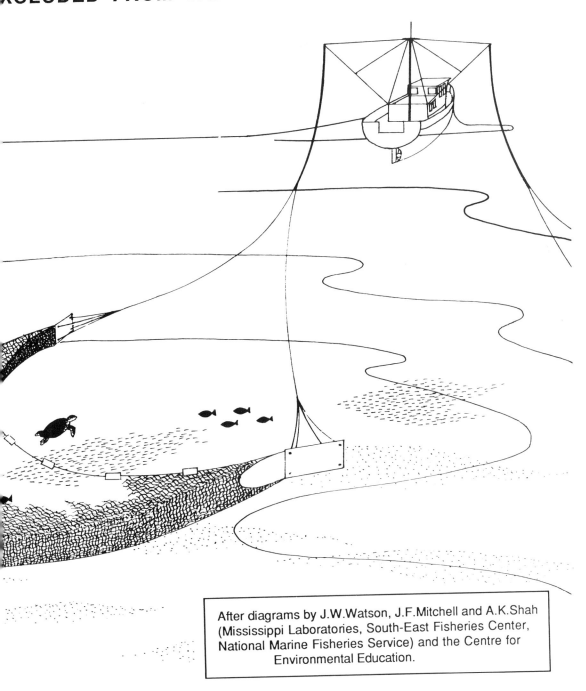

After diagrams by J.W.Watson, J.F.Mitchell and A.K.Shah (Mississippi Laboratories, South-East Fisheries Center, National Marine Fisheries Service) and the Centre for Environmental Education.

TURTLE EXCLUDER DEVICES

Turtles caught in trawl nets cannot reach the surface to breathe. A turtle can hold its breath for about an hour and a half, so it will usually survive if a net is lifted within that time, though often exhausted and in a state of shock. Thousands of turtles, caught in trawls that were towed for a longer period, suffocated (see *the diving reflex* below) in the days before turtle excluder devices, or TEDs, were used. It is unfortunate that major shrimping areas off Florida, Louisiana and Texas are also important feeding grounds for the Kemp's ridley. The shrimp share the habitat of the ridleys' favorite food, the blue crab.

Estimates, projected from samples, indicate that before 1987, when regulations requiring the use of TEDs were passed, more than 12,500 sea turtles suffocated each year in shrimp nets throughout the south-eastern coastal states, 5,500 of them in the Gulf of Mexico. Nearly 770 Kemp's ridleys were killed in one year. Shrimp fishermen also netted ten pounds of finfish for every pound of shrimp, and threw most of the finfish away. Every year they actually discarded five times the weight of groundfish caught by commercial groundfishermen, whose livelihood depended on the fish.

TEDs are sometimes called trawling efficiency devices because they let not only sea turtles, but also finfish, jellyfish, sharks, rays and sponges escape, without losing more than a small fraction of the shrimp. The forerunner of these devices was the Cameron Excluder, which was invented in Cameron Parish, Louisiana, to exclude "cabbage-head" jellyfish from the catch. At present three main varieties of TED are in use. The NMFS design, which features a metal grill and a trapdoor in the top, is the most effective both at allowing turtles to escape and excluding unwanted finfish. It is also the heaviest and the most expensive at $400 and up (or $200 for a do-it-yourself kit). The Georgia TED (or "Georgia Jumper") was designed by a shrimp-boat Master called Sinkey Boone, a colorful character whose sons are also shrimpers. It features an oval metal grill in the throat of the net, with a slot in the netting through which a turtle can escape by diving downwards. It is less effective at excluding finfish, unless the grid spacing is much reduced, but has the advantage that it will also exclude large floating objects such as oil drums. The "soft TED" was invented by Sonny Morrison, another shrimper. It is made from netting alone and, at less than $50, is one of the least expensive. It is effective for large turtles, though possibly not for small ones, and there is some concern that sharks might become entangled in the netting structure that corresponds to the metal grill of the other designs. The other officially sanctioned soft TED is the Parrish TED, designed mainly by net-maker Steve Parrish. The Morrison TED ejects turtles and debris out through the bottom of the trawl; the Parrish TED excludes the same items through the top. There is no doubt that all five of the designs already approved for use will be subject to

Box continued

modification and improvement in future, but it is important to emphasize that the present designs do operate as intended, and workable TEDs are available at the time of writing (late-1988). The NMFS has studied and tested TEDs for ten years, at a cost of more than a million dollars, to ensure that they really are practical, workable devices. Present versions are small, lightweight and collapsible. NMFS is currently putting observers aboard Gulf shrimpers, at least until the end of 1988, to collect data for a study of the economic impact of the TED regulations and to compare the performance of different kinds of TED under various conditions. The results of this study are due to be reported on or before January 1990.

The TED regulations are to apply between March 1 and November 30 each year to all shrimp trawlers. In offshore waters, trawlers 25 feet long or longer must use TEDs. Trawlers less than 25 feet long are not required to use TEDs if tow-times are limited to ninety minutes. In inshore waters (within the COLREGS DEMARCATION LINE — roughly fifteen miles or less from shore) all trawlers must either use TEDs or limit their trawls to ninety minutes or less.

The new TED regulations have still to be properly tested: the belief is that they will help to save sea turtles from extinction, reduce the time shrimp fishermen need to sort their catches, and save billions of pounds of finfish each year. Initial reports from Florida are very favorable, with shrimpers using Georgia and soft TEDs reporting no significant shrimp loss because of the use of the TEDs, and several sightings of sea turtles in the process of being excluded.

The diving reflex, possessed by some marine vertebrates, is an involuntary response to being submerged. The air passage in the throat is automatically shut off by a sphincter, which prevents water from entering the lungs and makes it impossible for the animal to drown. This is why turtles caught and killed in shrimp trawls are suffocated rather than drowned. The diving reflex has been suggested as a possible mechanism for the unexplained "crib deaths" of human babies.

A shark bites a piece off José's carapace.

XXII At Large In The Atlantic

JOSÉ AND TIMOTEO had been more venturesome. They hitched a ride on a raft of sargassum and drifted in the Loop Current around the Gulf of Mexico into the Florida Current, through the Florida Straits, and out into the Atlantic Ocean. For several months they drifted northward in the Gulf Stream, feeding on small sargassum creatures and growing larger. Eventually, large eddies bore them out of the stream and over the continental shelf toward the many food-filled bays and salt-marshes along the eastern seaboard. By mid-summer they had almost reached Long Island Sound.

While they were over deep water off Block Island, a six-foot tiger shark cruised stealthily up behind them. Timoteo saw it coming and darted off to one side, but José's response was not quick enough. The shark was suddenly upon him. Its powerful jaws, with their multiple rows of overlapping teeth, narrowly missed his moving hindflipper and snapped a large chunk out of the rear edge of his carapace.

José's rate of paddling suddenly increased dramatically. He spurted away in an evasive spiral and the shark lost track of him. Fortunately the wound did not bleed badly enough to leave a trail of blood. The pain burned for a time, then gradually faded, but the wound would take weeks to heal and the scar would remain for many years, perhaps forever. Following cautiously behind Timoteo, José swam in towards the shallow waters of the sound, where he would feel safer. Crabs and mussels thrived in the eelgrass along the coast and the two turtles began to forage happily.

They had arrived at the height of the fishing season, when fish weirs and traps are set along the coastline in shallow water and constitute another kind of hazard for turtles, though not generally a lethal one. This time it was José who stayed out of trouble, but more by accident than by good intentions. One day Timoteo did not pay enough attention to where he was going and was gradually guided into a trap by a fence of netting. Finding no way out of the enclosure, he swam around slowly in company with a school of herring that had also blundered into the trap. It was late the next morning before the fisherman came along to harvest his catch, and it was not the first time he had caught a turtle. He grumbled continually about unwanted regulations and federal government interference with honest fishermen while he was making a note of Timoteo's tag number. He would have to report it to the Okeanos Ocean Research Foundation, which would in turn report it to the NMFS Laboratory in Miami. Then his manner altered and he became extraordinarily gentle as he lifted Timoteo with one hand on either side of the carapace and placed him carefully back in the water outside the net. Timoteo floated on the surface for a second, then dived and disappeared in a trail of bubbles.

Timoteo and José spent the rest of the summer enjoying the crabs, shellfish, and other abundant food along the New England coast. In the fall, when the weather grew chilly, it was time to swim south to warmer waters, but either they lacked the right instinct or they failed to heed its prompting. As the temperature of the water dropped they gradually became colder and colder, until one day they became too numb to move and they were washed ashore, "cold-stunned", to lie helplessly among the seaweed and storm-wrack.[17] There they remained until they were found next morning by a beach-walker. Well-wrapped and muffled against the biting wind, she was one of the team of volunteers who look for chilled turtles along the northern Long Island shore during winter, especially after severe storms.

While José and Timoteo were being gradually revived in the relative warmth of a kiddie-sized swimming pool, their tag numbers were noted for another report to the Miami NMFS laboratory. They were fortunate both to have been found quickly and to be spending the night inside the small Jamesport house of Sam Sadove, Director of the Okeanos Ocean Research Foundation. The temperature outdoors fell far below freezing and any turtles left on the beach stood no chance of surviving. José and Timoteo revived so well that they kept everybody in the house awake that night by splashing enthusiastically with their flippers.

By morning the walls of the warm-up room were running with salt water and their hosts were happy to let them depart. They were placed in a box on moistened foam rubber and flown first-class from MacArthur Airport on Long Island to Miami, Florida, where they were released into Florida Bay, off the Gulf of Mexico.

COLD-STUNNING

The Okeanos Ocean Research Foundation organized weekly beach-walks after only eleven of forty-three cold-stunned Kemp's ridleys found on the beach in 1985 could be revived, and only four out of twenty-seven in 1986. The following year it rehabilitated six of the twenty-seven ridleys found.

Although the air becomes chilled, the water in protected bays stays warm until December, and turtles remain in the bays for longer than they should. When the bay water finally cools and they do try to leave, they encounter still colder water, begin to slow down, and finally become stunned.

Ridleys and other species of sea turtle are regularly found cold-stunned along the New England coast down to Long Island, New York, with most occurring in the New York region. The Okeanos Foundation rescues an average of 25 to 30 ridleys a year from Long Island beaches. About 5 to 10 a year are rescued at Cape Cod.

"Deaths from cold-stunning also occur in shallow estuaries on Florida's central east coast," says Larry Ogren. "The cold fronts that pass through these areas in winter can lower the water temperature rapidly. Escape to deeper and warmer waters offshore is blocked by long barrier islands."

"When there are a couple of very cold years, say every fifteen years or so, the sea can become cool enough for large-scale cold-stunning to occur even in Florida," adds Richard Byles. "One year 141 sea turtles — loggerheads, greens and one ridley — were rescued in Florida, and almost all survived after being revived in a warm, freshwater pond."

Box continued

Llewellyn Ehrhart and his students rescued these turtles in Mosquito Lagoon and Indian River on the east coast during the winter of '76 - '77. They found that about half of them had shells smeared with lagoon mud. "Lew" Ehrhart suggested that turtles may be driven to the bottom of the lagoon during severe cold and for some reason may fail to lodge there. (See the box on Hibernation.)

The fictional visit of Timoteo and José to Mr. Sadove's home is based on a true episode involving wild ridley turtles. Seven of the cold-stunned wild ridleys that have been revived have been flown back to the Gulf of Mexico from the New England-New York area. In connection with the fictional travels of José and Timoteo, David Owens advises us that there is very little indication that sea turtles are social, except during mating and arribada nesting.

The itinerant pair were lucky to be tagged, head started turtles, because they were returned to their home in the Gulf of Mexico. Four wild turtles, that had been found in pound nets or revived after cold-stunning, had small radio and sonic tags attached to their carapaces by Okeanos. They were then tagged, released the following summer near where they were found, and tracked in the Atlantic during the six warm months in the hope of determining whether they could return to the Gulf.

Dodging shrimp trawls, the two seasoned air-travellers swam cautiously around the coast to the mouth of the Mississippi and tried hard to lead a quieter, less eventful life. A number of their head start class-mates were already there. Now that they had abandoned the surface-feeding life and were spending most of their time on the bottom, the color of their carapaces had changed to a drab and muddy olive-green and the spotting had disappeared from their yellowish plastrons. They blended with the mud or sand and were hard to see from above. Before long they would be joined by an aloof cadre of adult turtles, many of them scarred and barnacle-ridden veterans, newly returned from their annual migration to Rancho Nuevo.

HIBERNATION?

Says Ogren: "Turtles caught by the cold in coastal waters of the United States have three choices. They can:

- Migrate southward to subtropical waters,

- Move offshore to deeper, warmer waters (or ride with the Gulf Stream either to cross the Atlantic or be dumped into even colder water along the northern U.S. coast), or

- Hibernate on the sea floor in deeper waters.

Migration is a popular choice, according to the NMFS, fishermen, and other observors, but little is known about offshore wintering, or hibernation, and both need further study. Scuba divers have reported lethargic loggerheads occupying deepwater Atlantic reefs off the Georgia coast in winter and fishermen report seeing active loggerheads at the surface along the western edge of the Gulf Stream in winter months.

"Dormancy occurs when the water temperature drops below 15deg C.," says Ogren. "If the temperature continues to fall, and if a suitable bottom type and depth for hibernation are lacking locally, cold-stunning or immobilization and death occur. The lethal temperature is below 8deg C."

Richard Byles explains: "Usually turtles burrow into the mud and hibernate when it gets too cold for their normal activities. When the temperature drops even further, they pop up from the mud and float. They can't swim, and breathe sluggishly, and a lot succumb to kidney damage from the intense cold."

Counters Ogren: "This may not be the case. If the turtle is a successful hibernator it would not necessarily pop up from the mud. Archie Carr, Charles McVea and I believe that they usually hibernate offshore in deeper (warmer) waters. Cold-stunning usually occurs in shallow water."

Fishermen told Carr and David Caldwell in 1956 that some sub-adult ridleys passed the winter buried in the bottom along the central Gulf Coast of Florida. Then, in their 1973 monograph, Pritchard and Márquez noted that turtle fishermen of the time on the Gulf Coast of Florida, particularly at Cedar Key, remarked that ridleys disappeared in the winter and reappeared in spring with their shells covered with mud. Pritchard and Márquez suggested that those that failed to embed themselves in time would be the ones that drifted across the Atlantic, in a more or less inactive state, to the coast of the British Isles and Europe.

The many juveniles found stranded on the coast of the British Isles, and less frequently on the Atlantic coast of Europe, are usually cold-stunned. Strandings are most numerous in the late fall, peaking in December.

Box continued

Two shrimp trawlers dislodged 81 feeble and listless immature logger-heads within the space of an hour from the muddy bottom of the 15 meter-deep Port Canaveral Ship Channel late in 1977. Some were smeared with a black substance that was probably anoxic bottom mud and the shells of others were partly mud-covered and partly encrusted with barnacles. The shrimpers concluded that the turtles had been partly buried in the mud for a long time.

Carr, Ogren and Charles McVea Jr. visited the channel to investigate in mid-February of the following year. Making test tows with a trawl, they disinterred 57 torpid loggerheads. Ogren and McVea then made a twenty minute dive, but found nothing because visibility on the bottom was less than a metre. On other dives they found that the temperature ten inches into the mud was nearly identical with the body temperatures of the turtles, and higher than that of the water, so hibernation seemed to be proven.

On a second trip to the channel in mid-March, the biologists caught three sub-adult ridleys and 97 loggerheads These turtles were more active, apparently because they were beginning to emerge naturally from hibernation. At this time the biologists saw many other turtles surfacing to blow with clouds of mud spreading around them. Two still had stacks of mud on their backs, and another had on its head a conch the size of a teacup, which remained there during two successive surfacings. Many of these turtles had fractured carapaces and peeling scutes, possibly the result of impacts by "transient vessels or trawlers".

The NMFS is searching for sites of group hibernation in natural depressions of the seafloor in south-eastern coastal waters. These will be mapped so they can be designated as critical habitats and protected from disturbance by trawlers and other traffic. In the winter of 1978-79, trawling was banned in the Port Canaveral navigation channel to protect the overwintering loggerheads. The only other gathering of torpid sea turtles reported overwintering in North American waters was at Baja California, Mexico. This population of green turtles has been severely depleted by divers who overfished dormant turtles during the winter.

F.J. Schwartz reported that chilled turtles held captive in shallow concrete tanks eventually become totally passive and float at the surface, tail-up, helplessly buoyed by intestinal gas. In mid-February, 1978, a trawler captain reported about 200 such derelicts, most of them badly mutilated, floating 38 miles out from the Canaveral Ship Channel. After investigating, Carr, Ogren and McVea suggested that these turtles had been dragged out of the bottom by trawlers after the water temperature had become too low to allow them to resume normal activity. After that they had probably drifted aimlessly, unable to feed and without the energy to evade shark bites.

Tina nests at Padre Island.

XXIII   The Return To Padre Island

ABOUT THE YEAR 2000 — turtles do not pay much attention to the calendar — Tina, José, Juanita and Timoteo find themselves together again, living comfortably on the Louisiana coast. Now they are fully-grown Kemp's ridley turtles, nearly thirty inches long overall and around eighty-five pounds in weight. Their carapaces, heads and flippers have lightened to an attractive grey-green color with olive-green tinges, and their plastrons are a soft, creamy gold. José and Timoteo have grown tails with curved, hard, callused tips that extend beyond their carapaces, and the curved nails on their foreflippers are elongated and very strong for gripping the carapaces of their mates.

They all feel the same strong urge to migrate, but not to Rancho Nuevo. An implacable instinct directs them, together with the other surviving members of their head start class, back to the Padre Island National Seashore where they were imprinted as hatchlings. It is a class reunion, of a highly unusual kind. They travel as a slow-moving armada, swimming during the day and resting on the waves at night, until one day they find themselves at a place which they somehow recognise as being the right one. Tina mates for the first time in the dawn light, floating offshore in a daze for several hours while her mate, whose carapace has a rakish, free-form shape with a bite-shaped piece missing from the rear edge, remains grappled firmly to her back. Some days later[18] she swims purpose-fully to the shore. She emerges from the surf late on a windy morning in May and is sighted first by a beach-walker and then by a ranger on roving patrol. The two watchers remain quietly by the dunes so as not to disturb her while she begins her long, pre-programmed crawl up the sand.

When she is a safe distance above the high-tide line, Tina first excavates a large, shallow pit for her body, and then begins to dig her nest, using a technique that has been refined and standardised by more than a hundred million years of repetition. While Tina is preoccupied with stretching each hindflipper alternately into the sand to scoop out a hole for her eggs, Juanita has just begun to crawl out of the sea a little farther along the beach, and a dozen other turtles at various stages of nesting can be seen on the same quarter-mile stretch of shoreline. When the excavation is complete, Tina enters a trancelike state and begins to lay her eggs.

As soon as egg-laying is under way, the ranger approaches quietly from Tina's rear, careful to stay away from the turtle's head and out of her field of view, and notes the position of the white, living tag on her carapace that identifies her year class, the lack of any major scars, and the absence of a flipper tag, which has long since been corroded or worried away. The little magnetic wire is still there in Tina's left flipper, but the reading it gives on the magnetometer tells only that the turtle was head started. The ranger puts the magnetometer back in her pack and uses a tape to measure the length and breadth of Tina's carapace. Then she takes out a portable scanner and uses it to read the code stored in the passive inte-grated transducer (PIT) that remains embedded in Tina's shoulder after all these years and is still in working order. Tina's unique code identifies her and links here with the mother who abandoned her as an egg on the Rancho Nuevo beach more than a decade earlier.

While the ranger is taking several photographs to document Tina's return for her files, Tina finishes laying, covers and tamps the nest by thumping with her shell while rocking from side to side, and rotates laboriously, making several partial turns in succession, and using her front flippers to distribute sand over the nest site and the two people.

Then she turns to begin her trek back to the sea and the ranger hurriedly takes the new, non-irritating, plastic tag that has just been extruded by the versatile PIT-scanner and clips it onto Tina's left foreflipper. Tina seems about to object, but fatigue outweighs indignation and she is satisfied to continue plodding back to the ocean.

As Tina disappears under the waves, the ranger digs up the 65 eggs (an average clutch for a first-time nester), slips them into a biodegradable plastic bag and carefully ferries them over the dunes on her venerable beach bike to the new hatchery building. There one of Donna Shaver's successors puts them into a box for incubation, alongside other boxes already holding clutches of eggs. After hatching, some of the little turtles will be imprinted in the usual way, and then will travel to Galveston to form a new head start class, just as their mothers did more than ten years ago. The others will be released at Padre Island to fend for themselves.

The numbers of Kemp's ridley sea turtles in the Gulf of Mexico and along the Atlantic coast of the U.S.A. are increasing steadily and once again many hundreds of turtles nest in a day at Rancho Nuevo, thanks to the years of protection of turtles and eggs at Rancho Nuevo and Padre Island and to the fact that TEDs are compulsory on both United States and Mexican shrimpboats. Significant populations of nesting turtles have begun to be reported at other protected nesting sites along the Gulf coast. Perhaps in a few decades the nesting of Kemp's ridleys at Padre Island may come to equal the extraordinary arribadas of olive ridleys at Costa Rica — described as one of the wonders of the modern world — but with the advantage of being much more readily accessible to nature lovers in the U.S.A.

Because the head started turtles are returning to nest at Padre Island, there is no reason to bring an annual supply of eggs from Rancho Nuevo. Instead, eggs are exchanged between the two colonies to help maintain the gene-pool. The Galveston laboratory is head starting hatchlings from the Cayman Turtle Farm and releasing them at various locations. The international teams at Padre Island and Rancho Nuevo devote their spare time to research, in the intervals between checking the tags of nesting turtles, transplanting eggs into corrals, releasing hatchlings into the sea and maintaining a continuous watch for hurricanes, oil spills and junketing VIPs. And at Rancho Nuevo, the Marines remain on guard.

Tina, graceful once more now that she is back in her natural element, rejoins the squadron of Kemp's ridley turtles that are waiting beyond the breakers. Only a trail of flipper prints and a patch of twice-dug-over sand betray her visit, and windblown grains are already erasing the prints.

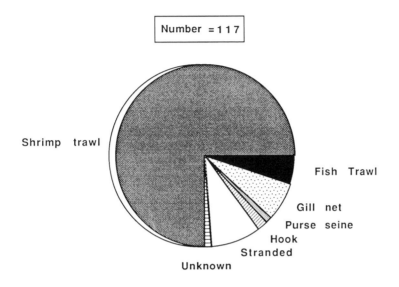

METHOD OF RECOVERY OF KEMP'S RIDLEY FEMALES
TAGGED AT RANCHO NUEVO, MEXICO.
1966 - 1986

Number = 1 1 7

Shrimp trawl

Fish Trawl

Gill net

Purse seine

Hook

Stranded

Unknown

(Data from Márquez)

XXIV Hazards To Sea Turtles

THE SEA CAN BE A DANGEROUS PLACE, especially if you are small and edible. Here we consider only man-made hazards to sea turtles. These are of two kinds — accidental and intentional. Taking the accidental hazards first, the main risks in this category for a turtle are:

- Suffocation in shrimp trawls.
- Injury by hook and line fishermen.
- Coating by, and ingestion of, oil and tar from spills, seeps, oil rigs and ships. Tarballs can drift into rafts of sargassum or be washed up on nesting beaches, where they can stick to the plastrons and flippers of nesting turtles and of hatchlings making their way to the sea. Hundreds of yearlings from the '82 year class were oiled and washed ashore, dead, at Padre Island soon after their release. Some of them had actually eaten the oil.

• Ingestion of plastic bags or other plastic trash such as Styrofoam packing pellets, and non-plastic debris. These materials eddy around in the currents with the sargassum weed and are caught up with it and eaten by turtles. The turtle either chokes or suffers a gut blockage.

• Shock from underwater explosives, used to sever the legs of petroleum platforms in salvaging them from depleted oil fields in the Gulf of Mexico, may injure or kill turtles in the vicinity of the explosion. Any oil company contemplating such a removal must alert the Minerals Management Service and NMFS. Procedures to monitor the removal are developed in consultation and NMFS observers must be present during the removal. If sea turtles are seen, operations are postponed until it is safe to blast.

• Entanglement in crab and lobster pot lines and in fishing nets. Turtles may survive net capture and can be released by the fishermen. Any large-meshed net, such as a gill, pound or drift net, can entangle a turtle. In its struggles to free its neck or flipper it may wrap the net so tightly around itself that it cannot reach the surface to breathe, and suffocates. The problem disappears if a smaller mesh size is used.

PLACE OF RECAPTURE OF HEAD STARTED KEMP'S RIDLEYS
1978-86 YEAR CLASSES

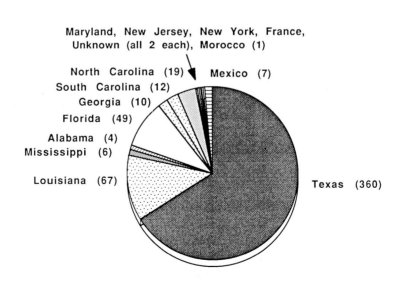

Total = 547

Maryland, New Jersey, New York, France, Unknown (all 2 each), Morocco (1)

North Carolina (19)   Mexico (7)
South Carolina (12)
Georgia (10)
Florida (49)
Alabama (4)
Mississippi (6)
Louisiana (67)   Texas (360)

(Data from NMFS Galveston Laboratory December 31 1987)

• Entanglement in man-made materials in the ocean. These gradually weaken the turtle and can cause it to starve or be vulnerable to predators. Biologists have reported turtles washed ashore, dead, after dragging around for an unknown length of time such materials as large sheets of plastic, ropes, crab or lobster pots, or netting.

Other reported causes of death include collision with a boat propeller and being sucked up by a dredge that was deepening a channel. Propeller injuries are a relatively common occurrence in certain areas, notably southeast Florida. Regulating boat speeds in areas of high turtle population could help, and dredge dragheads can be modified. It is speculated that turtles are also killed by ingesting chemical wastes.

After 1966, when Kemp's ridley was protected from poachers and predators at its Rancho Nuevo nesting beach, the high incidence of death by accidental capture in shrimp trawls remained an intolerable burden on the species. The compulsory use of TEDs by shrimpers is expected to eliminate this hazard. American shrimpers have been required to use TEDs from March 1988. However, TED regulations were temporarily enjoined from enforcement from April 12, 1988, because of a federal court injunction relating to an appeal based on a lawsuit filed by the State of Louisiana. (Supporters of the effort to save the ridley have organized a shrimp boycott in retaliation for the injunction.) On July 11, the Fifth Circuit Court of Appeals dismissed the injunction against enforcing the TED regulations, the dismissal to become effective at midnight on August 31, 1988. Enforcement of the TED regulations, from Texas to North Carolina, has been postponed until 1989, or until 1990 in the case of inshore waters, pending reauthorization of the Endangered Species Act.

The extent of the damage is proven. Márquez found that, between 1966 and 1985, nearly 75 percent of recaptured Kemp's ridleys that had been tagged at Rancho Nuevo were taken in shrimp trawls, and one suspects that this percentage might have been significantly higher if every captured turtle had been reported.

Pritchard, who found that most of the tag returns from both the Kemp's and olive ridley populations were reported by shrimpers, noted that in many cases the turtles were not returned alive to the sea. According to Hildebrand, the number of reports from fishermen who accidentally catch the species has diminished considerably since the present law on endangered species was introduced. (This, in turn, hinders tagging programs studying migrations and mortality.)

Capture of sea turtles in shrimp trawls is actually one of the major causes of strandings, the NMFS Galveston Laboratory concludes in its 1987 report. Discussing the 533 head started turtles recovered from 1978 to September, 1987, it says that nearly a quarter of the turtles (124) were reported by shrimpers or port agents as having been caught in shrimp trawls and 70 percent of these 124 turtles were reported as alive after release from the trawls, a surprisingly high figure. A further 100 turtles release from the trawls, a surprisingly high figure. A further 100 turtles were discovered stranded alive and another 131 were found stranded dead; the implication is that many of these stranded turtles had become stranded after being released or discarded from shrimp trawls. Larry Ogren notes that the large number of subadult wild ridleys recorded stranded during the past few years have frequently been found in areas adjacent to the shrimp fishing grounds and at the onset of the fishing season.

In two studies where dead, tagged sea turtles were set adrift from shrimp trawlers, only 4 out of 13 were later found stranded (G.F. Ulrich) and only 2 out of 9 radio-equipped loggerhead carcasses became stranded (T.M. Murphy). Thus the dead, stranded turtles found in shrimp fishing areas are probably only a small fraction of those killed at sea.

HEAD STARTING AND TEDS

Head starting and hatchery conservation can be used as excuses for exploiting turtles, or for abandoning other conservation programs that are known to be effective but are more difficult to implement. So writes Dr. Jeanne A. Mortimer, one of Archie Carr's students, in *Florida Defenders of the Environment - Bulletin 25* (May-June 1988).

She explains that U.S. District Court Judge Patrick Carr of New Orleans, when noting in April 1988 that the Kemp's ridley would become extinct in about twenty years at the present rate of decline, went on to say: "However, head starting programs or hatcheries are being utilized to increase the population of the Kemp's ridley.... Therefore, a delay of a few months pending this appeal will not substantially harm any species of sea turtles."

Mortimer notes: "Despite his recognition of the species' plight, he was influenced by the notion that the benefits of turtle hatchery and head starting programs are sufficient to compensate for damage caused by the shrimping industry. The National Oceanic and Atmospheric Administration interpreted the ruling to apply to all shrimpers from North Carolina to Texas. This delay in implementation of the TED rules will result in the loss of more turtles, and it leaves them unprotected for the remainder of this year's shrimp season."

She emphasizes that head starting cannot be considered a proven management technique until it has been demonstrated that head started turtles will eventually breed on appropriate nesting beaches, and that their rates of survival and successful reproduction are greater than those of wild turtles. No head started turtle has ever been observed nesting, so there is no proof that head started turtles will eventually reproduce.

The U.S. Fish and Wildlife Service and the NMFS regard head starting as still very much an experimental technique. Because it is experimental, Pritchard

Box continued

pointed out in 1979 that it should never be used as a justification for higher levels of harvest of wild turtle populations, or conducted to the exclusion of direct release of hatchling turtles.

Nevertheless hatcheries and head starting programs have been used repeatedly to justify exploitation, as Mortimer explains:

"At the District Court hearing, Louisiana's Assistant Attorney General, E.R. Megginson, who represented the shrimpers, suggested that 'the TEDs regulation ... is the wrong alternative... because all it is going to do is save a few turtles.' With the support of the shrimpers, she proposed that, instead of requiring the use of TEDs, a tax be levied on shrimping licences 'in order to raise money for head starting programs which would stock the populations.' Unless the shrimpers use TEDs, however, large numbers of these head started turtles will end up dead in shrimp trawls."

"We do not know how, or even if, imprinting occurs in turtles," Mortimer writes. "Will a turtle that has never been imprinted to a beach even try to nest? If so, perhaps it will choose a beach that is inappropriate for the survival of its offspring. Another possibility is that turtles which have not been properly imprinted might disperse over so great an area that they are nowhere concentrated enough to breed successfully.

"The Galveston turtles are generally released off the Texas coast in the open sea. Although it is hoped that their brief exposure to the elements as neonate hatchlings is sufficient to imprint them to the nesting beach, as yet there is no evidence one way or the other that this is so. Imprinting, if it occurs, might be a far more complicated process that requires longer exposure to sensory cues. For example, it is conceivable that imprinting might occur during the 'swim frenzy' — that period lasting 3 or 4 days after a turtle hatches from its egg and during which it swims continuously in a direction approximately perpendicular to the shoreline.... During the swim frenzy the hatchling might be exposed to a variety of cues involving such stimuli as odors in the water currents, polarized light, magnetic fields, or low-frequency sound waves."

She also mentioned other unresolved problems about head starting. While some head started turtles were recovered in healthy condition after months or years at sea, others were found dead or in very poor condition within weeks after release. Some were easily captured near land, possibly because they associated people with food. Also, an unnatural diet and lack of exercise could weaken the turtles. The concerns expressed by Pritchard in 1980 were still relevant:

"Should they be treated as 'big hatchlings,' and released on their natal beach to crawl into the sea and enter the same currents that they would have entered as hatchlings? Or should they be released in places where similar-sized wild individuals of the species already occur? In the absence of any good knowledge, one might guess that the first technique might favor imprinting, but the second survival.

Box continued

131

"There are a lot of things that could go wrong, and at this stage the most sensible precaution is to submit only a small percentage of the hatchlings from a given beach to the head starting process," Pritchard wrote.

"When head starting is advocated as a solution to the survival problems of turtles, the public can be lulled into believing that no other protective measures are needed," Mortimer warns. "The expensive hatcheries and headstarting programs can create a false sense of optimism about the future of the species, when their long-term benefits to the turtles have still to be proven.

"Although it is satisfying to rear and release baby turtles, we must be careful not to neglect the less glamorous and politically more difficult, but less experimental and - in the long run - probably more effective tasks of passing and enforcing protective legislation, raising funds for habitat purchase and educating the public," Mortimer concludes.

(Charles Caillouet comments: "Undoubtedly, Dr. Mortimer's statement that no head started turtle has ever been observed nesting refers to head started turtles released in the wild, because head started Kemp's ridleys have been observed nesting in captivity, even when as young as 5 years old, at Cayman Turtle Farm (1983) Ltd., B.W.I. No hatchlings produced by the 5-year-olds survived, but the same group of turtles nested successfully and produced hatchlings when 7, 8 and 9 years of age. This indicates that Kemp's ridleys can mature and reproduce at quite an early age, at least in captivity, and gives hope that their head started counterparts released into the wild would not be far behind in age at maturity and nesting. Nestings also have been observed in 6-year-old head started Kemp's ridleys held in the captive stock at Clearwater Marine Science Center, Clearwater,Florida.")

Threats to Habitat

Coastal development, ocean pollution and other activities not intentionally directed at the turtles can result in loss of habitat, and the development of coastal wetlands can destroy the habitat of the ridleys' food animals. These are serious long-term threats to many species, not just to individual turtles.

Other threats to the habitats of sea turtles include damage to the sea floor, and especially to sea-grass beds, by dredging and filling operations, by improperly operated shrimp trawls or even, in some places, by the anchors of pleasure-craft. Damage to coral reefs affects hawksbills, greens and loggerheads. For the Kemp's ridley, the most vulnerable point is clearly the primary nesting beach at Rancho Nuevo, which is susceptible to damage from an oil spill or a hurricane. Experience has already shown that an oil spill is particularly dangerous during the nesting and hatching season. But much more serious in the long run is the way that the sea itself is becoming a less satisfactory environment for all species, including ourselves, as a result of steadily increasing pollution by oil, tar, sewage, industrial wastes, and miscellaneous trash.

Strandings of hundreds of sea turtles on beaches bordering the Gulf of Mexico each year are symptomatic of something radically wrong in the coastal ecosystem of which the turtles are a part, according to the NMFS Galveston Laboratory's annual report for 1987. Either man's at-sea activities (such as shrimping) or major changes in the sea turtles' natural environment, or both, are stressing the turtles and causing their mortalities.

In 1986 Archie Carr wrote, in connection with his investigations of the time spent by young sea turtles in rafts of sargassum weed, that the "...pelagic stage is much more protracted than initially believed, and during this time the turtles are brought into intimate contact with concentrated marine pollution. Growing awareness of the steady spread of marine debris and pollutants, of the tendency of these to collect along frontal driftlines, and of the habit of hatchlings to eat virtually any small object within reach, made closer investigation of this phase of sea turtle life seem urgent."

To give an indication of the pace of change, we recall that in 1979, when the Rancho Nuevo hatchlings were released by helicopter at the time of the IXTOC oil well blow-out, they were dropped off near a large raft of sargassum because this was their natural hiding and feeding place. Ten years later, NMFS staff avoided releasing head start hatchlings near floating patches of sargassum, for fear that they would ingest or be coated by the tar that the sargassum now traps and accumulates.

Reduction and ultimately elimination of all kinds of pollution of the sea, which covers the greater part of our planet and affects in a fundamental way the lives of every species in the world, must become a major concern of us all for many years to come.

It remains to consider the deliberate killing of sea turtles. Although it is against the law in most countries where it has been customary in the past, people still sometimes eat turtle eggs and kill turtles to eat the meat or turn it into soup, extract the oils, make the skin of the neck and foreflippers into luxury leather goods such as handbags, wallets, boots or shoes, and use the shells for decoration or fashion them into jewellery. This is a continuing serious pressure on hawksbills. There is a large, mostly illegal, international trade in turtle products, many of which find their way to Japan and Europe. Fortunately, there is an increasing tide of public opinion against this kind of exploitation of rare wild animals, and with continuing pressure on consuming countries this unsavoury trade may simply wither away.

As Charles Caillouet points out: "Were there no market for turtle goods, pressures to exploit turtles would subside. The consumer of such goods, knowingly or not, is an accomplice in the killing of the animals and shares in the demise of sea turtle species that are part of our natural wildlife heritage."

In the United States it is illegal to tamper with a nest or to take or possess any sea turtle or any portion of any sea turtle, including eggs, shells or skeletal remains, without federal and state permits. Offenders can be fined up to $20,000 and spend up to a year in prison. Rewards of up to $2,500 are offered for information leading to the arrest and conviction of persons killing or otherwise molesting turtles.

Today, fewer than 600 turtles, representing essentially the total population of mature female Kemp's ridleys, nest along the 20-mile stretch of beach at Rancho Nuevo during the three-month nesting season. Because of this critical situation, captive stocks of the turtle are being held in several aquariums. Delay in the introduction of the 1987 federal law requiring all Gulf shrimpers to use turtle excluder devices in their nets might well have resulted in more fatalities than the species could endure.

HILDEBRAND ON TEDS

"In many visits to Rancho Nuevo, I never found any hard evidence of a significant slaughter of adults, though I heard and saw reports of it," says Professor Hildebrand, "but nowadays, with the small population, every mortality is of concern. The use of turtle leather in Mexico did not begin prior to 1964 and I doubt that it had a significant role in the decline of the Kemp's ridley. This brings us back to egg predation and accidental capture as the principal causes. Either one alone could have caused the decline, but together they were devastating. The size of the largest arribada recorded by Chávez in 1966 — 1,500 turtles — reflected the extent and effect of the egg predation in the 1950's and 60's.

"Protection of the nesting ground at Rancho Nuevo has been adequate since 1978, when the United States became a partner in the Mexican preservation program that began in 1966," Hildebrand says. "However, despite more than twenty years of protecting the turtles, eggs, and hatchlings from natural and human predators, the number of nesting females continues to fall.

"Turtle biologists conclude there is a large loss of turtles from accidental capture in fishing gear, particularly shrimp trawls. Kemp's ridleys migrate annually to Rancho Nuevo from their favorite feeding grounds along the upper Texas and Louisiana Coasts in the north, and in the Bay of Campeche to the south. The northern route is trawled intensively by shrimpers from Louisiana to Rancho Nuevo. A smaller fleet of trawlers, and hectares of rough, untrawlable bottom, greet the turtles from the south.

"United States shrimpers have tried to sidestep the regulations for the compulsory use of turtle excluder devices by blaming the Mexicans for the drop in turtle numbers. Although a share of the blame belongs to them, the Mexicans had a protective program in operation before we did and I think that should be recognized," Hildebrand says.

XXV Invitation To Take Part
In A Survival Project

On JUNE 13, 1985, a beachgoer at Padre Island saw a nesting ridley turtle and did not disturb it, but marked the nest site after the turtle had returned to the sea and reported the nesting to the National Park Service. They collected the eggs and incubated them. Sixty-three hatchlings from these eggs were raised in the 1985 head start class at Galveston and were called the "the Texas Sesquicentennial Kemp's Ridley Sea Turtles". One was named "Lone Star" by Carole Allen, who had the honor and pleasure of releasing it off Mustang Island from the U.S. Coast Guard Cutter "Point Baker".

The first recorded Kemp's ridley nesting at Mustang Island since 1962 was watched, by Carlton J. Miller, as she laid 104 eggs on April 27, 1988. Miller flagged down a passing motorist, a Neuces County worker, who notified Miller's oceanographer friend, Tony Amos. Assisted by Pam Plotkin, Amos captured the turtle, confirmed it was a ridley and took its measurements. The eggs were incubated at Padre Island National Seashore, producing 95 healthy hatchlings after 57 days, and the hatchlings were set free at the nest site on June 25. Miller told the *Corpus Christi Caller Times* that he and Amos often drove along the beach together, and that he had done so frequently over the last thirty years because he was "always interested in seeing strange things on the beach."

You too can help safeguard the survival of sea turtles. Watch out for live or dead turtles on the beach. If you see one, follow the advice given in the next few pages. Even if you don't remember the Alamo, remember Lone Star. Here is how you can help:

• Get acquainted with some turtles. Visit during the open houses at the NMFS Laboratory in Galveston in the first half of February or in May, or telephone to arrange for a group or school tour. Visit marine aquariums that have Kemp's ridley and other sea turtles on display. At

Padre Island National Seashore, join a ranger for an interpretive beach walk at 7 a.m. on one of the July mornings when there is a chance to observe imprinting of hatchlings at Closed Beach, and possibly the opportunity to help as a turtle watcher or net wielder.

• Work with HEART to save the turtles. Contact HEART to learn how to adopt a turtle, to join HEART, or to form a HEART council. (See Have A Heart And Save A Turtle later in this book.)

• Keep watch for turtles on the beach. By the end of 1987, 231 stranded head started turtles, 100 of them still alive, had been recovered and identified. In 1987 alone, 590 wild sea turtles of different species were found stranded on the Gulf coast and 1,766 on the Atlantic coast of the United States.

• Support the work of conservationists, such as those at the Center for Environmental Education, when they try to reduce the amount of pollution and trash in the sea and on the beaches. Assist them in their fight to protect the environment and to help endangered species of animals and plants to survive. Nearly 160 tons of marine debris were collected in three hours by 4,522 volunteers during the Great Texas Beach Trash-Off on April 23, 1988. (Reported by the *Center for Environmental Education — Galveston Daily News*, July 8, 1988). Early analysis of the trash showed that more than 60% of it was plastic.

What to Do if You Find or Accidentally Catch a Sea Turtle

If you catch a turtle on a hook or in a net while fishing, remember that such turtles can usually be released unharmed. If the turtle has not swallowed the hook, you can try to remove it (watch out for bites). Do not try to remove a swallowed hook; instead, report the turtle immediately to one of the agencies mentioned opposite.

If you find a turtle on the beach it will either be nesting or have been washed ashore injured, sick, cold-stunned or dead. Healthy sea turtles rarely leave the sea. In some places, an occasional turtle will bask in the sun near the water's edge.

If the turtle is nesting, do not touch or disturb it, or it may go back to the sea without laying its eggs. If left alone, it will go through the whole routine of crawling up the beach, making a body-pit, digging a hole, flinging sand into the air, laying eggs in the hole, filling it in, tamping it flat, scattering sand around, and then heading back to the sea. The National Park Service (NPS) patrols the length of the Padre Island National Seashore (PAIS) from mid-April until mid-July, looking for female head start turtles from the early years of the program, which may now be mature and returning to nest. However, as PAIS is 70 miles long and large areas often have no park service personnel on them, it is most important that visitors keep a lookout for nesting turtles and tracks and report sightings to the service.

If you see a nesting turtle, do not disturb her. If possible, fetch a ranger quickly. Otherwise, wait until she is laying eggs, then approach carefully from behind and see if there is a tag on a front flipper. Please record the tag number, take photographs if you can of the top view of the turtle, the nesting activity, the crawl, and the tag, if any, and mark the nest location after the turtle leaves. Photographs are very helpful for identifying the species and documenting the nesting. If no ranger is available, also measure the carapace length and width. To report your data to the Ranger Station Staff at Padre Island National Seashore, telephone (512) 949-8173 or (512) 949-8068.

If the turtle is injured, sick, cold-stunned or dead, note its location and its apparent condition and report it immediately to one of the following institutions: the National Marine Fisheries Service (NMFS), the U.S. Fish and Wildlife Service (FWS), the NPS (especially at the Padre Island National Seashore), the Texas Parks and Wildlife Department (TPWD), other state conservation agencies, coastal oceanariums, or marine biology or oceanography departments of coastal universities, who usually participate in the Sea Turtle Stranding and Salvage Network.

If it is an unusual hour or there is no answer, call the local NMFS or TPWD Law Enforcement office. Reporting even a found shell provides useful information, but remember to leave it where you found it, because possession of any part of a sea turtle can lead to a fine of up to $20,000 and a prison term, and the enforcement agents are extremely serious-minded people.

What to Do if You See a Tag on the Turtle

If you find a turtle that has a metal or plastic tag on any of its flippers, or a radio or sonic transmitter unit, or a single light spot (a "living tag") on its carapace, please report it as described below to the NMFS Miami Laboratory, Florida, as well as to one of the agencies already mentioned, such as a ranger station if you are in a national park. The Miami laboratory keeps release and recapture records of tagged turtles, as well as records of strandings.

If the turtle is alive, leave the tag in place. Note the number, return address, position on the turtle and type of tag, and also the date and the location of the turtle. Record any other information about the sighting, stranding, or accidental capture and, if possible, a measurement of the carapace length, taken in a straight line from front to back. Again, photographs would be valuable for aiding identification. Report the information as soon as possible to:

Cooperative Marine Turtle Tagging Program
NMFS Miami Laboratory
75 Virginia Beach Drive
Miami, Florida 33149
Telephone: (305) 361-4200

Release the turtle into the water if it seems healthy; otherwise notify one of the agencies as soon as possible so they can recover the turtle for rehabilitation.

If the turtle is dead, remove the tag and mail it to the address on the back of the tag, or to the Cooperative Marine Turtle Tagging Program at the address above, together with the same information as listed before for live turtles and a description of the condition of the carcass. Also, write the number of the tag in the accompanying letter. It is very important to mail the tag in a strong envelope, or have the envelope hand-cancelled, so that the tag will not rip through the paper during postmarking by an automatic franking machine. Many tags have been lost in this way and often the tag number was not given in the covering letter.

"Tags are a critical part of our research and recovery programs," says biologist Barbara Schroeder of the NMFS Miami Laboratory. "One tag return can produce an enormous amount of information about a recaptured turtle's growth, migrations and survival."

The Sea Turtle Stranding and Salvage Network

Barbara Schroeder is national co-ordinator of the Sea Turtle Stranding and Salvage Network (STSSN). The network, which has its headquarters at the NMFS Miami Laboratory, arranges for the eastern and southern coasts of the United States, and portions of United States territories in the Caribbean, to be patrolled for stranded turtles. It documents and where possible salvages any turtles found. Approximately 12,000 stranded turtles, representing five different species, were reported from these beaches by STSSN members in the seven years up to 1987. During 1986 alone, 1,846 marine turtles were found stranded in the region.

Pairs of graduate students use beach bikes to cover thirty-mile stretches of coast in Texas, south-western Louisiana, and Mustang Island, and National Park Service personnel patrol the Padre Island National

Seashore. The Fish and Wildlife Service and the Texas Parks and Wildlife Department patrol Matagorda Island. Biologist Marcel Duronslet of the NMFS Galveston Laboratory, who coordinates the patrols in this area, reported 180 stranded Kemp's ridleys in 1986. Texas stranding coordinator for the STSSN is Robert Whistler of the National Park Service (Padre Island National Seashore); the Louisiana coordinator is Steve Rabalais.

TED letters from Orchard Elementary School.

XXVI Have A Heart And Save A Turtle

"**A**DOPT A TURTLE AND SPONSOR ITS CHOW for ten months by writing to HEART, P.O. Box 681231, Houston, Texas 77268-1231. Either send a $4 donation or buy a ridley turtle marionette, T-shirt, turtle pillow/toy, raisin' ridley cookie cutter, painting, or tote bag. An extra dollar helps pay for the hatchling's yellow bucket. Your name will be written on a red plastic heart and pinned on the wall of the turtle house at Galveston."

Who could resist such an appeal! We couldn't.

"You may wish to join the organization or form a HEART council with members of your family, club, scout group or school class, or with your friends," says Carole Allen, Chairperson of HEART. "Each council has an adult sponsor and in turn sponsors at least five hatchlings."

Members of a HEART council have the opportunity to view the outstanding video cassette *The Heart-break Turtle* and, if they are in the Houston area, see a slide show and hear a tape about American sea turtles. Mrs. Karen Stockton of HEART travels around the Houston area, presenting the ridley story to various organizations. It is described as a very moving performance, with slides, music and quotes from books by Archie Carr and a poem by Tim Fontaine.

"Council members are encouraged to write to their congressmen and senators in their home state and in Washington D.C. to ask them to continue voting for money for sea turtle conservation, and to find out what their legislators are doing to enforce the Endangered Species Act. The first of the present eighty councils was formed by pupils from Oak Creek Elementary School."

HEART has played a significant part in removing the largest remaining hazard to ridleys. In 1987, after an intensive campaign by HEART supporters and many others, Congress affirmed that in future all shrimpboats must use TEDs. Carole and her daughter Jane were among the speakers at a crucial federal hearing early that year, and arrived armed with petitions signed by 5,000 HEART members and supporters from throughout the country.

Charles Caillouet has designed a marionette of a Kemp's ridley sea turtle yearling, called "Kempy", which can swim or crawl very realistically. (The turtle's scientific name is Lepidochelys kempi.) HEART sells the plans and directions for its construction, or the precut and painted turtle kit, and all proceeds go towards sea turtle conservation, with Caillouet retaining the copyright. Caillouet also designed the raisin' ridley cookie cutter, which was named by his wife Nancy. Of the cookie cutter, Carole says:

"I finally found a cookie cutter company that would make it but they demanded a minimum order of a hundred dozen. Against the advice of some I forged on and have found it to be a big money maker. I had stacks of cookie cutters in the guest room for a long time — now I'm down to just a few hundred."

Carole formed HEART in 1982, after the head start project began, and has been its Chairperson since then. Her main aims were to educate people about ridley turtles, invite them to Galveston to see the turtles, raise money to support the program, and assist in any way possible. Now she leads a committee of six who work with the students, teachers, scout leaders, conservation organizations, herpetological societies, science clubs and thousands of individuals who are interested in the turtles. HEART is sponsored by the Piney Woods Wildlife Society — the nature club of North Harris County College (Texas) — and receives strong support from herpetological societies.

"HEART supplies and sends educational material to thousands of people and groups, mainly in the U.S., and Pat Burchfield distributes it to the children of Rancho Nuevo," she told us. Funds raised by HEART helped build the United States barracks at the turtle camp at Rancho Nuevo and paid for a beach bike. They also covered a large proportion of the cost of the new turtle hotel at Galveston. At present the organization is trying to obtain field supplies and used vehicles for Mexican turtle biologists and volunteers. Not long ago, Pat Burchfield travelled to Houston to accept a truck that had been donated through HEART and take it back for use at Rancho Nuevo.

Whether fighting tirelessly at federal level for the use of TEDs, or against inhumanity to turtles at any level, Carole Allen retains the sense of humor that keeps her brown eyes sparkling. Time and again she has helped rally the nationwide forces of turtle conservationists and direct their attention to the latest crisis. In 1987 she graduated with a degree in journalism from the University of Houston, at the same time as Jane graduated from high school. Jane's work on turtle conservation helped qualify her for the award of a community service scholarship.

Carole rehabilitates stray or injured turtles, and sometimes birds, raccoons, opossums and armadillos. People from all over Houston bring her turtles they have found on roads or in their yards, or telephone for her to collect them. If the turtle is sick, she first takes it to the veterinarian and then nurses it back to health in her greenhouse, which has a dirt floor for box turtles and plastic swimming pools for water turtles. She has had up to twenty-five turtles in residence at the same time and admits to a liking for all kinds of turtle, even the alligator snapping variety.

When I visited her at home, during Houston's relatively mild winter, they were all inside the house for warmth. A saucer-sized "yellow-bellied slider" fresh-water turtle with an infected plastron was sitting for an hour in a sulfa solution and receiving regular antibiotic injections. Five tiny box turtles (also called tortoises), each the size of a quarter, and a pair of two-inch box turtles, crawled around in two foot-square plastic containers set on warming pads under a greenhouse lamp.

"You have to keep the little ones warm so they won't hibernate. The little guys will go to sleep all right if they cool down, but they don't always wake up again. At this age it's a lot safer to make them think it's still summertime."

Carole has collected turtle knick-knacks of all kinds since she was a small child. There are turtles everywhere, on end tables, on the walls and in shadow boxes. The theme is sustained from the front door mat to the kitchen wallpaper. Her mother, Golde Hoover, who was visiting for Christmas, gave me one of the attractive pictures of Kemp's ridleys on a Texas-shaped background that she paints to raise funds for HEART.

"I've loved turtles since I was five and living in Illinois," Carole told me. "My brother brought home a little water turtle and that was it. It's not just the sea turtles that I like and want to help, but all kinds — even snappers and stinkpots. If it has a shell, I like it. I raise them until they are safe and then release the box turtles at a friend's ranch near Buffalo and the water turtles at Lake Conroe or Lake Houston. Turtles are wild and deserve to be free and away from people because people disturb them. I become very attached to them and find it hard to let them go, but eventually I release all the turtles that can cope with the natural environment.

"Their problems are created by humans — traffic and a loss of habitat for the land turtles, and trawling nets, exploitation and pollution for the sea turtles. I want to improve the situation for them. It's up to those of us who care to help them."

Carole Allen receives a certificate from Dr. Edward Klima.

143

"Carole Allen is extraordinarily impressive," says Peter Pritchard. "On first meeting her you might think that Carole is an attractive housewife in her mid years, say to yourself 'what a pleasant woman', and go no further than that. But a little more contact and you realize this is a serious underestimation. She is very competent and capable in getting things done.

"She has learned a great deal about ridleys and their survival and she not only knows how to get the support of the citizenry of Galveston — both adults and children — for the support of the ridleys, but she also knows all the points in the government system at which pressure should be applied and writes very good letters directed to those points. She has become an excellent turtle biologist, public relations specialist and lobbyist. Without her, Operation Head Start would have faltered years ago for lack of government funding. HEART raised the funds when there wasn't any money to feed the turtles. She is a modern-day Dearl Adams."

In 1984 Edward Klima presented a certificate of appreciation to Carole for meritorious support of Kemp's ridley sea turtle recovery. Carole also received the National Wildlife Rehabilitators Association's Special Achievement Award in 1987.

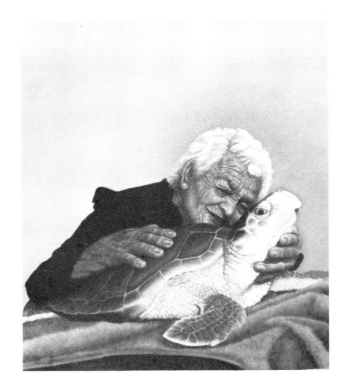

*The Turtle Lady of Padre Island,
Ila Loetscher, with Jimmy Junior.*

XXVII The Turtle Lady Of Padre Island

AFTER ILA LOETSCHER had taken part in Dearl Adams' egg convoys in the nineteen sixties, she set up a kind of rest home for sick or injured turtles that people brought to her. It began in 1966 with three small turtles, called Winkin', Blinkin' and Nod, that Adams asked her to care for after he had hatched them on Padre Island. The idea was to watch them grow to maturity and so determine how long it would take the rest of the brood to mature to the point where they might return to Padre Island.

At first the turtles were kept in a wading pool behind her house in the little town of South Padre Island. In 1967, after hurricane Beulah had left her with just four walls standing and no roof and the turtles had to be given a temporary home in a Corpus Christi aquarium, she had corrals constructed for them nearby in Laguna Madre. Many of her charges were no longer fit to survive in the wild and soon she had a small, permanent collection of turtles, covering a range of different sizes and species. Later, when five became ill and died during construction of the Laguna Madre Bridge, she moved the others into wooden tubs in her house. Six years later she had concrete tanks with rows of seats above them built in the back yard of her new home and began to give turtle shows.

It was at Professor Hildebrand's suggestion that she began a turtle awareness program to foster a love of sea-turtles among school children. At first she telephoned schools and visited them, but soon the schools asked to visit her, and people were coming to her house in steadily increasing numbers to see the turtles in her care. At first she would not accept any contributions toward the turtles' upkeep and did everything by herself, but the number of visitors continued to increase until it was obvious that something would have to be done. Sea Turtle Incorporated, a non-profit corporation, was set up in November 1977, to receive income from Ila's turtle shows and distribute it in support of research on the reproductive physiology of sea turtles. She now asked for a minimum contribution of one dollar from anybody over the age of four.

"Ila's Sea Turtle Incorporated is a voluntary organization very like HEART, and took the place of HEART in the old days," David Owens told me. "It has provided a lot of funding for my research. One year, for example, it gave a substantial grant that allowed me to take four students to Mexico for a month of field work. Now it has set up a development fund through Texas A&M University to support my Kemp's ridley research work."

Now in her eighties and after overcoming health problems that would send most folk into early retirement, Ila is giving up to seven turtle shows a week for school children during the spring, and two shows a week for tourists and the general public. She gives extra shows for people who drop by. Before we arrived, Ila had taken an unscheduled nap because thirty people had visited her the night before and she had just given two turtle shows in 90-degree temperatures. On the next day, Sunday, which was her day off, she would devote the morning to preparing coffee for various congregations at her church.

David Owens regularly takes blood samples from Little Fox, Ila's seventy-pound female Kemp's ridley. Measurements of hormone levels in the blood can, amongst other things, establish whether a turtle is male or female with a high degree of certainty. (Ila believes she can guess a turtle's sex with an accuracy that rivals the blood test.) Texas A&M's Department of Biology uses Little Fox as an example of Kemp's ridley reproductive maturation in its long-term studies of the captive breeding of Ila's turtles. Owens, a Professor of Biology, has been on the faculty of Texas A&M University since 1978. In his early forties, quiet, athletic, and balding, he is described as a gentleman who is first and foremost an academic scientist, researcher and teacher. Although he is deeply concerned about turtles, his evident scientific detachment makes him a key witness in Washington where, according to Carole Allen:

"Congressmen see him as an objective scientist who hasn't been tainted by me!"

"When we go there," says Owens, "Ila insists on holding Little Fox on her lap while we take the blood sample. She gets into the tank in her wetsuit and lifts Little Fox to the surface. Then we hold the turtle while she jumps out of the tank, and we place it in her lap. The turtle is probably heavier than she is. It struggles when we lift it out of the water but becomes quiet as soon as it's on her lap. She talks to it and holds its flipper all the time and it lets us take the blood sample without even flinching. The first time I saw this I had to believe and admit that this animal recognized her and responded."

"I always call a turtle after the person who brought it to me," said Ila, rubbing the throat of an appreciative and friendly female Kemp's ridley. "That's why she's called Jimmy Junior — after the shrimper who caught her in his net. He rang the Coast Guard first, and brought her to me the next day. She was only ten inches across then.

"Jimmy Junior adopted Smiley McCoy, who was found on the beach with malformed vertebrae and a collapsed lung. Smiley was expected to live only a year, but Jimmy mothered her by lifting her to the surface to breathe whenever necessary and Smiley's shell bent inwards to compensate for the uninflated lung. When a turtle comes here sick, the others are very kind to it and will take turns to lift it up to breathe."

Dr. Porter, her primary male for breeding, crossed the border illegally in an egg in 1976. The details remain obscure. The offender took him to Ila because a sand crab damaged a flipper after the egg hatched. Dr. Stuart Porter, formerly chief veterinarian at the Gladys Porter Zoo, repositioned the bone. At the time of our visit the turtle Dr. Porter was away breeding at an aquarium. In his absence, his tank was being repainted light blue by Ila's helper, Reuben Ruiz.

DR. PORTER RETURNS

Dr. Porter and Little Fox mated on May 20, 1988, in the presence of about fifty camera-equipped tourist bureau representatives.

"What a frenzy of interest this caused!" wrote Evelyn Sizemore, co-director and photographer for Sea Turtle Inc. "I was out of town, but all too many cameras were there to record the event."

When no eggs had appeared by June 19, Owens and his group did ultrasound examinations and were disappointed to find that Little Fox had not ovulated. Little Fox was then injected with a hormone to stimulate her pituitary gland. This procedure, which has been successful with other captive animals, was also used with six captive females at Sea-Arama Marine World in Galveston. On July 7, Donna Shaver wrote to say that 39 eggs laid by Little Fox were being incubated at Padre Island National Seashore. "Ila and her group were so happy when the turtle laid the eggs!"

Jerry, an Atlantic green, had been found cut, bruised and bleeding, after waves had dashed him onto rocks near the jetty.

"They click when they're sick. You hold them in your arms, they put their head on your shoulder and they just keep clicking. You click back and they love you from then on," the Turtle Lady explained, nursing him tenderly. "Are you going to make some noises for momma now? (Click, click .... ?) No, not while people are around."

Geraldine, another Atlantic green, arrived with a tar ball stuck in her throat after she had eaten a fish embedded in tar. Ila kept poking lettuce down her throat until the blockage cleared.

"The three children who brought her in to me named her after their grandmother. I hope she appreciates the honor," Ila said with a smile. Lieutenant Eddy, also an Atlantic green, had choked on a Styrofoam coffee cup. He was dropped off by a Coast Guard patrol plane piloted by a lieutenant of the same name.

Hazel, a ten-inch loggerhead, was only five inches long when she arrived. A fish-hook had lodged in her flipper and she had spent a long time on the end of the line. Fortunately the line was long enough for her to reach the surface to breathe.

"You couldn't put down a dear little turtle like that," said Ila, showing us Hopalong, a 2-year-old head start ridley with a collapsed lung on one side and a tumor on the other. Hopalong was swimming contentedly around his tank in small circles. Dave Irene, a green turtle in the adjacent tank, had been named for both Dave Owens and Ila's twin sister.

The irrepressible Ila, who once put three small live ridleys on a dampened cloth in a coffee can with holes in it and sent them to Professor Carr by air freight, now has fourteen turtles in her care. She enjoys going around the turtle tanks, clambering over the lids or sitting on top of them, and feeding her friends with small chunks of squid held in tongs. To control the water temperature, she lifts off the heavy wooden lids in the evenings in summer and in the mornings in winter.

"Nearly 25 years ago Ila became deeply involved in a project to enhance the survival prospects of the ridley turtle," says Professor Hildebrand. "In her own way she has developed a very effective publicity campaign on the plight of this species, as well as all species of sea turtles.

"Tourists as well as local Valley residents enjoy the turtle shows at her home and go away better informed. In addition she has appeared on several national television shows, including Johnny Carson's Tonight Show. She and her co-workers have collected a lot of useful information about sea turtles in South Texas."

Gentle and kindly Evelyn Sizemore has been Ila's friend for twenty years and co-director and photographer of Sea Turtle Inc. since 1978. She is a very effective, self-effacing worker behind the scenes. When asked about her membership of the 99s, an international organization of licensed women's pilots, she quickly said that she only flies occasionally now from a local field, and mentioned that in 1927 Ila was the first licensed woman pilot in the state of Iowa. Evelyn also said:

"Ila has found out more about the personalities of sea turtles than anyone thought possible. She is a devoted and dedicated person."

A 1987 National Conservation Achievement Award of the National Wildlife Federation was presented to Ila in New Orleans in March, 1988, after she had been nominated for the award by Carole Allen.

We leave the last word to the legend herself:

"I love being the Turtle Lady of Padre Island," she said, her eyes shining. "I wouldn't be anything else."

TURTLES AND POLITICS

Dedicated individuals like Carole Allen and Ila Loetscher play a vital role in protecting endangered species. One of their most important functions is to help bridge the communication gap between professional biologists and the public, and they increase public awareness of non-economic issues relating to the real need to prevent the extinction of any endangered species, whether it be a sea turtle, a bald eagle, a brown pelican, a whooping crane, a grey wolf, or some obscure creature that only a conservationist could love.

Conservationists believe, with justification, that mankind is diminished by the loss of even one species from the world, however insignificant. Whether or not they agree with this view, an informed public is better able to vote or lobby for conservation issues and provide a counterweight for the purely economic arguments that always find ready spokesmen.

The fate of Kemp's ridley, and of the Endangered Species Act itself, were in jeopardy at the end of 1987, when the act came up for reauthorization by the United States Congress. Special interest groups were attempting to attach weakening and delaying amendments to the act. The Kemp's ridley turtle was the focus of long and bitter discussions when the shrimp industry lobby battled for an amendment to postpone compulsory use of TEDs in the Gulf of Mexico for another two years. In the end, because both the informed public and the conservation organizations made their voices heard, the amendments were defeated in the House of Representatives.

The defeat of the amendment to delay the introduction of TEDs was " . . . . the most significant wildlife conservation vote by the House this decade," wrote Congressman Gerry E. Studds, Chairman of the House of Representatives Sub-Committee on Fisheries and Wildlife Conservation and the Environment, in a letter to Carole Allen.

At the time of writing, the battle is still not over. The delaying injunction, from an appeal against the decision in a lawsuit by the State of Louisiana, has already been mentioned. Also, the reauthorization of the Endangered Species Act has still to be acted on by the U.S. Senate. A number of influential senators have written to Department of Commerce Secretary William C. Verity (defendant in the State of Louisiana's lawsuit) asking for further delays. Many more turtles will be killed in shrimp trawls before the smoke clears.

"Tampering with the Endangered Species Act affects all endangered animals and plants; this (the TED issue) is not a turtle issue, it is a bald eagle issue and a whooping crane issue and a piping plover issue," writes the Houston Audubon Society's Vice-President for Environmental Affairs, Jane Scheidler, in *the Naturalist* (May, 1988).

Box continued

The basic issue seems to be whether or not short-term economic factors should be a consideration when the survival of an entire species is at stake. Conservationists point out that once a species is extinct it is lost from the earth, never to be seen again. They question whether this is a price the world can ever afford to pay for some short-term economic gain. It is now widely accepted that uncontrolled environmental effects of human activity, such as those associated with large public works projects like dam construction or river diversion in the public sector, or thoughtless property development in the private sector, should not go unchecked. Threats to the survival of endangered species are more and more often the consequence of such enviromental impacts. The debate becomes more complicated when a change in long-established custom is advocated for environmental reasons, but recent legislation dealing with smoking in public places shows that here too the wider public interest can win.

In the case of the Kemp's ridley turtle, there is a mass of evidence which shows that continued shrimping without the use of TEDs would contribute significantly to extinction of the species, despite all the dedicated work that has been done and is being done to save it. The requirement to use TEDs may cause the price of shrimp to the public to increase slightly, to compensate for the additional capital costs to the shrimper, costs arising directly from the public's desire to perpetuate the existence of the Kemp's ridley turtle. Most consumers of shrimp would not begrudge this. However, the turtle lobby points out that the NMFS TEDs' elimination of large finfish from the catch, with a consequent saving of fuel and time spent sorting the catch, ought to offset much of the extra expense. And despite the rhetoric, there seems to be no truth in the rumor that TEDs might cause shrimpers themselves to become an endangered species.

Dorsal view of the Kemp's Ridley, Lepidochelys kempi.

From an article: European Atlantic turtles, by L.D. Brongersma (1972) plate 10. Zoologische Verhandelingen Nr. 121, courtesy of the Rijksmuseum van Natuurlijke Historie, Leiden, The Netherlands.

XXVIII About Turtles

TURTLES HAVE BEEN ON THIS PLANET for a very long time. The amphibian ancestors of all reptiles left the sea to live on land about 185 million years ago. In contrast, the hominoid ancestors of modern man appeared only about four million years ago. Turtles were among the first reptile species to evolve. Those that we call sea turtles moved back to the sea at the time of the dinosaurs, 150 million years ago, producing, in Archie Carr's words, "... such multi-ton monsters as *Archelon*, with a twelve-foot flipper spread, and *Meiolania*, with a horned skull two feet wide." Those we call box turtles or tortoises remained on land, while those called terrapins became adapted to living both on land and in fresh water.

Of sea turtles, it is normally only the adult females that ever leave the sea. They crawl ashore to nest for about an hour at a time, often several times in a nesting season. (Rarely, ardent males pursue them onto the beach.) Later the newly emerged hatchlings scurry over the beach from the nest to the water. Except for these brief periods, sea turtles spend their entire lives in the ocean.

Today eight species of sea turtle can be found in the oceans and seas of the world,[20] primarily in tropical or subtropical areas. Most are in danger of extinction. They have been killed in the past, and in some places are still being killed, for their meat, oil, skin and shell, and their eggs have been gathered for eating. Every year thousands have been accidentally captured and killed in shrimp trawls, in other fishing nets, or by hook-and-line fishing gear.

Five species — loggerhead, Kemp's ridley, green, hawksbill and leatherback — inhabit the Gulf of Mexico. The adults range in size (defined as average carapace length) from the 24-inch ridley to the 6-foot leatherback. All five species are also found on the Atlantic seaboard; the olive ridley replaces Kemp's ridley on the western shores.

Turtles are reptiles. This means that they are 'cold-blooded' (the temperature of their body varies with the temperature of the surrounding water or air), that they have a backbone and scales and breathe air, and that the females lay eggs with parchment-like or brittle shells. Some species may mature in less than 10 years; others take up to 30 years. Some tortoises are reputed to live 150 years or more and some sea turtles to about 100 years, but experts regard these figures as speculative and probably exaggerated.

Sea turtles cannot retract their head and feet into their shell in the way tortoises and most terrapins do. Protection has been sacrificed for powerful muscles in neck, shoulders and swimming limbs. The feet of sea turtles have been modified into flippers for swimming.

Kemp's ridley sea turtle, Lepidochelys kempi, the rarest and almost the smallest sea turtle in the world, is the species in greatest danger of extinction. In forty years the number of nesting females at Rancho Nuevo has fallen from as many as 40,000 in one day in 1947 to fewer than 600 in the entire nesting season of 1987. It differs from other sea turtles in that its carapace is almost circular and, like that of the Australian flatback, flatter than those of most other species. As with the loggerhead, its head is larger and broader than one would expect for a turtle of its size.

"If it's as wide as it is long, and it's olive green in color with a big head, I'd say you've got Lepidochelys kempi, the Atlantic ridley - Kemp's ridley..." said Archie Carr, when Jack Rudloe, author of the book *Time of the Turtle*, telephoned him to ask the name of a turtle he had found.

COLOR AND AGE

"The color of Kemp's ridley changes several times from hatchling to adult, and I don't think many people are aware of this," says Ogren. "The Cajun fishermen tell me that in some places, such as Terrebonne Parish, Louisiana, some folks call this turtle the 'black' turtle. They have shown me young, post-pelagic ridleys eight to eleven inches long with a black carapace."

After hatching, the turtle looks dark grey when dry and black all over when wet. The carapace and upper skin surfaces remain black as the carapace length reaches 4 to 11 inches, but the plastron and its adjoining skin become white or light cream. Juvenile Kemp's ridleys typically have three elevated 'keels' on the dark carapace.

As the turtle grows larger, the carapace gradually fades to light grey, becoming olive-grey in adulthood, and the plastron becomes a light tone of yellow ochre. When the turtle is very old, the carapace reverts to grey. At each of the later stages of development, the upper surfaces of the light skin on head, neck and flippers change to match the color of the carapace.

Changes in color with age are characteristic of Kemp's ridley (see box). The carapace can reach 27 inches in length, and its width is usually a couple of inches less, though it can be the same. Adults have been recorded weighing up to 108 pounds. Average adults have a carapace length of about 24 inches and weigh about 85 pounds.

Kemp's ridley has a cousin, the olive ridley, which lives in the tropical Atlantic and Pacific Oceans and tends to be slightly smaller in size. Whereas Kemp's ridley has five central plates, called 'scutes', on its carapace (vertebrals) and five pair of scutes on each side of them (costals), the olive ridley usually has six vertebrals and usually six to nine costals, though occasionally five. The olive ridley's carapace has steeper sides and a flatter top and is darker in color in the adult. The cousins are separated by the Caribbean. In the Atlantic, olives are found around Trinidad and eastern Venezuela, Guyana, Suriname, French Guiana, Brazil and rarely in Colombia, Cuba and Puerto Rico. They are still abundant in the eastern Pacific and Indian Oceans, although now under considerable pressure from exploitation. Kemp's and olive ridleys are the only species that have uniformly dark or black hatchlings.

Kemp's ridley is generally regarded as more aggressive than the other species and has the reputation of strenuously resisting capture. On the other hand, Rudloe says, in *Time of the Turtle*, that ridleys make the best aquarium pets (this was written before they were protected by the Endangered Species Act), being far more intelligent and responsive than the cumbersome loggerheads and having more personality than the docile greens or irritable hawksbills.

They feed mostly on the bottom in the shallow waters of the Gulf of Mexico, especially off Louisiana, West Florida and Campeche, and the eastern seaboard of the U.S.A., eating crabs, snails and clams, jellyfish, and, in the opinion of some biologists, plants.

"Kempi is generally thought to be a benthic carnivore, with a preference for crabs," says Larry Ogren. "Many items are accidentally or incidently ingested. This is the case with dead shrimp and fish that is discarded at sea as bycatch of the shrimp catch. I believe that shrimp aren't eaten by turtles (nor are fish, for that matter) because shrimp can avoid capture by 'kicking' rapidly away or by burrowing. Sometimes folks get the wrong impression that turtles are competitors with man for shrimp and fish. I don't think that is an accurate assessment. It may be physically impossible for a turtle to catch these critters. The plant items sometimes found in the stomachs of ridleys are probably the supporting structure edible molluscs were attached to."

(However, Charles Caillouet finds that Kemp's ridleys, being rehabilitated after being found stranded and barely alive on the beach, can readily catch live shrimp fed to them in captivity, albeit under less than natural conditions for both shrimp and turtle.)

Each spring the adults migrate to Rancho Nuevo, on the coast of Tamaulipas, Mexico, to nest from April to July, or occasionally August, returning afterwards to their feeding grounds. During a tagging program in 1968, Chávez found that the average distances swum away from Rancho Nuevo of the two fastest turtles in his sample were 15 and 18 miles per day. Apart from the large aggregation nesting near Rancho Nuevo, there are records of scattered nestings from Isla de Aguada, Campeche, to Mustang Island, Texas, the greatest numbers of reports coming from Tecolutla in Veracruz, and Washington Beach, Matamoros. Mating takes place in the waters off nesting beaches.

Hildebrand says: "Both the subadults and adults feed on the highly productive white shrimp-portunid (= swimming) crab beds of Louisiana and Tabasco-Campeche, Mexico. As with the nesting grounds, there is some leakage of individuals and small groups to other areas away from the primary sites. The reason for the popularity of these two areas is two-fold: they have the largest concentrations of the crabs in the Gulf, and the turtles are carried to both areas by the Gulf currents.

"When the young enter the current system at Rancho Nuevo, they are either transported northward by the western Gulf boundary current to the Loop Current in the north-eastern Gulf, or southward by an eddy. They are strongly attracted to the areas where river and sea waters mix at the mouths of the two major river systems of the Gulf — the Mississippi in the north and the Grijalva-Usumacinta in the south. The offshore drift lines of logs and other debris from the rivers provide hiding and feeding places for the young juveniles. In the north, most of the ridleys should be found around the delta and westward across Louisiana to the Sabine area of Texas. This area is extended westward during years of high river discharge.

"As they grow, the young move inshore during the warm months and offshore in the winter in the north Gulf. This pattern is not necessary in the warmer waters of the southern Gulf, but no information is available from there or at least not published. There is some leakage into the eastern Gulf and the small population of subadults off Cedar Key was commercially harvested until the early 1970's. There appears to be no doubt that the eastern Gulf population contributes to the nesting population at Rancho Nuevo, and it is expected that the tagging program now in place will confirm it."

PLACE OF RECAPTURE OF KEMP'S RIDLEY FEMALES
TAGGED AT RANCHO NUEVO, MEXICO
1966 - 1986

Number = 117

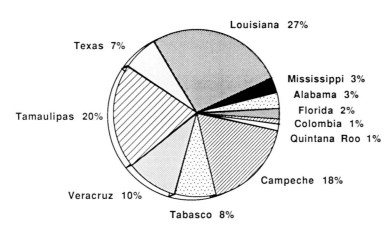

Louisiana 27%

Texas 7%

Mississippi 3%
Alabama 3%
Florida 2%
Colombia 1%
Quintana Roo 1%

Tamaulipas 20%

Campeche 18%

Veracruz 10%

Tabasco 8%

(Data from Márquez)

157

XXIX Migration Mystery

MYSTERY AND FRIENDLY CONTROVERSY still surround the migratory habits of the ridleys. Some biologists, led by Professors Hildebrand and John Hendrickson, have always believed that young Kemp's ridleys carried by currents into the Atlantic Ocean become waifs, lost forever. However they do not doubt the ability of the young turtles to swim back to the Gulf of Mexico.

Hildebrand says: "Because of the variability of the Gulf currents, in some years large numbers of young turtles are transported through the Florida Straits via the Gulf Stream. The sporadic nature of the records from the Atlantic Coast in the past certainly supports this contention. Most of the turtles which pass through the straits are probably lost to the population, but some may make it back to the nesting grounds. This seems possible if we consider the long migrations made by the olive ridley from the crab-rich grounds off Ecuador to nesting grounds in Mexico."

Ogren and Tyrrall Henwood take a more optimistic view of the fate of the Atlantic turtles and believe that a large proportion of the young ridleys survive over the winter:

"We suggest that the turtles forage as far north as Chesapeake Bay in spring and summer and migrate back to Florida (or farther south or west) in the fall to winter-over there. Seasonal movements up and down the coast may continue until they reach sexual maturity, at which time the turtles presumably return to the Gulf of Mexico to breed."

Rejection of the theory that the Atlantic turtles normally migrate back into the Gulf is based on the following evidence, as supplied by Hildebrand:

• All age groups — adults, sub-adults and juveniles — are found in the Gulf of Mexico and frequent the important feeding grounds in the Louisiana and Campeche-Tabasco areas. These grounds are large enough to support a Kemp's ridley stock of a size that could account for both the past and present breeding population.

• No tagged Kemp's ridleys other than head started turtles have been reported to have moved from the gulf to the Atlantic, and none have been shown to make the reverse migration. (Only cold-stunned, airlifted, wild turtles have returned safely.) No Kemp's ridleys tagged in the Atlantic have ever been reported or recaptured in the Gulf.

• If the migration were mandatory, as proposed by Pritchard and Márquez, there should be many records of ridleys from the Miami-Dry Tortugas area of Florida. Though the species has been reported from the Florida Keys, it has always been considered rare in those waters. (Woody points out, however, that this is not the only scenario for the migratory route.)

• Most of the Kemp's ridleys are found in northern waters and reported individually as cold-stunned or dead in New York and Massachusetts, as happens nearly every year. Possibly the healthy one- to five-year-olds that are found up the east coast and migrate southwards in autumn also die sooner or later from cold-stunning, because no adults or nesting Kemp's ridleys are ever seen along that coast.

Other biologists, led by Drs. Pritchard and Márquez, disagree, and present the following case for migration back into the Gulf:

"Very few immature ridleys are found south of Rancho Nuevo," says Pritchard. "They move north and clockwise with the current, settling down in suitable protected waters on both the Gulf and U.S. Atlantic shores. Those that reach Europe are almost certainly lost, but the U.S. Atlantic ones will grow and migrate southward in winter in normal circumstances, but always subject to cold spells if severe enough.

"It does not seem credible that so many would almost reach adult size and then die, and I prefer to believe that they move back to the Gulf before they mature. Very few have been tagged in the Atlantic, which would account for the absence of Atlantic-to-Gulf tag returns."

Members of this camp emphasize that cold-stunning and beaching is a rare event, even though at times it involves many turtles. They point out that there are large numbers of healthy, one- to five-year-old ridleys along the east coast and most of them migrate south in winter. Because these turtles are good swimmers and can hold their own easily against a three to four knot current, some may find their way back to the Gulf. The south-flowing alongshore counter currents (counter to the Gulf Stream) could move them along to Florida and they would then have to find a way around the southern tip of Florida. This should not be a difficult task for an animal with homing instincts.

Most of the younger, three- to four-year-old turtles are found in the north, around New England. Maybe they migrate south to winter off

Richard Byles holds a loggerhead sea turtle equipped with a satellite transmitter in Chesapeake Bay. The turtle probably lost its flipper in a shark attack.

Georgia or Florida, then travel north to the Chesapeake Bay area, where turtles a year older are found, before returning to the Gulf. Perhaps the nearly grown ridleys found at Cedar Key, on Florida's west coast, have returned there from the Atlantic. The other sub-adults which sometimes occur at places on the Atlantic coast, such as Brevard County, Florida, complicate things further.

"We have found there is a far greater presence of ridleys in our area than is indicated by the cold-stunning," said Sadove, of the Okeanos Ocean Research Foundation, New York. "The hundred or so pound-net fishermen each catch, on average, ten to twenty ridleys a year. We are now tagging every animal caught before releasing it into the Atlantic, and we plan to do some satellite tracking in a couple of years to find the direction in which they swim."

Professor Carr suggested that young loggerheads hatched on the south-east United States coast spend several years in the Atlantic, possibly crossing the ocean both ways before returning to live in coastal waters. Perhaps ridleys could do this as well? Tagging should provide the answer.

SATELLITE TRACKING OF SEA TURTLES

Backpacks equipped with transmitters were fitted to the carapaces of some nesters at Rancho Nuevo in 1988 so they could take part in a satellite tracking study of the Kemp's ridley. Whenever these turtles rise to the surface of the ocean to breathe, short antennas pop up from their packs to relay information about their behavior and movement to the Argos Satellite and thence to the Argos Data Center for computer analysis.

"Disturbingly little is known about sea turtle behavior and movements in the ocean, and this creates a significant void in our understanding of their ecology." says Richard Byles, who is both field project leader for this tracking study and one of the pioneers in the field. In 1987 the National Fish and Wildlife Foundation, Washington, D.C., awarded a research grant of $100,000 to the U.S. Fish and Wildlife Service to carry out the study.

"Assuming everything goes right, the transmitters should provide data for a year or longer," Byles continues. "Each will relay information about its turtle's location, dive times, depths, and annual and seasonal movements. In this way we should learn which habitats the turtle prefers and uses throughout the year."

Up to twenty adult female turtles should be equipped with transmitters before the end of the 1988 nesting season. Seven already had their units fitted by June 7. This is the first time a large number of sea turtles have been tracked by satellite simultaneously. Previous work involved one or two turtles, and usually they were the larger loggerhead species. The present effort must still be considered experimental.

The Fish and Wildlife Service can call up the Argos Data Center on their computers to receive the results. They may or may not get a "hit" from the animals every day, and they do not expect to get information about their location daily. This is because a number of requirements must be met for good location data to be recorded: the satellite must be at the right place in the correct orbit, and the turtle must be at the surface and must remain there for more than two minutes.

"Two types of transmitter housing are being tried," says Byles. "One is a backpack which fits on the forward part of the carapace with a short, six-inch antenna, and the other is a cigar-shaped cylinder which is attached to the trailing edge of the carapace by a stainless steel wire about 18 inches long. The transmitter is housed in the cylinder, with a short antenna that pops to the surface when the animal does. This antenna must clear the sea to transmit. Package weight, on land, is about two pounds."

While the United States mainly provided workers for the Rancho Nuevo effort, it could also assist with specific projects like the satellite tagging, which could not be arranged by Mexico, René Márquez commented. Mexico, assisted by the United States, would continue applying routine tags to the nesting females at Rancho Nuevo. In the twenty years to 1986, 4,120 turtles had been tagged in this way during the nesting season. From these, 117 tags had been returned. The place and method of recovery is shown in the pie diagrams on pages 157 and 127.

XXX Tagging Research

LARRY OGREN SAYS: "There are still large gaps in our knowledge about the development of sea turtles. We need to identify habitats which may be critical during certain stages of their lives and determine their seasonal migrations. The tagging and release of sea turtles captured at sea is still our best and most productive method of learning about the numbers and distribution of sea turtles in coastal waters and their seasonal migration."

For ten years, Ogren and Henwood have used this method to study immature Kemp's ridleys and green turtles along the south-eastern coasts of the United States, especially off Florida, Georgia and South Carolina. Most of the turtles are captured by shrimp trawls, strike gill nets, or turtle tangle nets. In some areas they are caught in pound nets or by hook and line, or after being immobilized by cold-stunning. Before the tagged animal is released the biologists record its species, condition and weight, and the date and location, and take several shell measurements.

"We are especially indebted to Captain Eddie Chadwick of the fishing vessel 'Mickey Anne' for resuscitating, measuring and tagging sea turtles from the bycatch," the biologists wrote in one of their papers. "His tagging effort significantly extended our knowledge of sea turtle migrations along the Atlantic coast."

Ogren continues: "Nothing is known about the distribution, or even the occurrence, of hatchlings in the pelagic stage in the Gulf of Mexico. A few are sometimes observed swimming in the surf zone off Padre Island, Texas, and some have been tossed up on the beaches of Mustang Island, Texas, during storms. In either case, the zone near the shore, with its attendant predators, is clearly not the appropriate habitat of these young turtles."

The problem of the location and lifestyle of very young sea turtles of all species, from hatchling to yearling, has been a mystery of long standing. In one of his last research papers, a NOAA technical memorandum dated 1986, Archie Carr wrote: "... it is now well-established that hatchling sea turtles go into sargassum driftlines if there are any within their reach.... Swordfishermen... repeatedly told us that in the area north-west of Little Bahama Bank... massive driftlines of sargassum form, especially in February and March. When this occurs, the fishermen say, little turtles 'the size of your hand' can often be seen on and among the mats in the weedline along which the swordfish long-lines are set."

We have already considered the likely effects of marine pollution on these young turtles under the heading of "Hazards to Sea Turtles, Threats to Habitat".

Ogren and Henwood collected the smallest benthic-stage juveniles, with carapaces 8 to 10 inches long, in depths of up to 3 feet in eastern Texas, western Louisiana, and Wakulla and Franklin counties in north-west Florida. Older juveniles were widely distributed in the coastal waters from Texas to Maine, with most occurring in the Gulf of Mexico. Almost all the turtles over 10 inches long that were captured in north-west Florida were in water less than 20 feet deep. Sub-adults up to 22 inches in carapace length were found foraging from Port Aransas, Texas, to Cedar Key, Florida, and sometimes off eastern Florida.

Along the east coast the average size of the turtles increases towards the south. This supports the idea that the very small ridleys, transported by currents from the Gulf of Mexico north to New England, ride shoreward across the continental shelf on large eddies from the Gulf Stream, leaving some of their number to continue with the current to Britain and Europe. In the eastern Atlantic, ridleys range in size from small post-hatchlings to large subadults. Mature turtles usually remain in the Gulf but a few adult-sized individuals have been recorded in the Atlantic.

"The juveniles remaining in the coastal waters of the eastern United States then migrate seasonally either between the New York bight and Chesapeake Bay and Florida, or offshore to warmer waters," Ogren says. "Only during spring-summer-fall have researchers found them inshore north of about latitude 29 N [near Daytona Beach, Florida]."

This theory is supported by the high concentrations of turtles which occur off Canaveral during the winter months — nearly all the Cape Canaveral ridley captures take place from December through March. Data on offshore movement to deeper and warmer water for northern Gulf ridleys is scanty and hard to obtain, but three juvenile ridleys were captured by a trawler at depths from 70 to 95 feet in late winter and early spring off Apalachicola Bay, south of Tallahassee, Florida.

The researchers find that the behavior of the turtles is not uniform. Some tagged turtles moved long distances (for example, 562 nautical miles in 202 days) and others short distances (37 nautical miles in 445 days).

However, we have no idea of the routes and area covered by the individual between capture dates, which could have involved a round-trip to Florida during the winter. One juvenile tagged at Cape Canaveral was recaptured in Virginia after travelling 200 nautical miles in 61 days.

Since the mid-1970s the largest numbers of turtles have been caught by shrimp trawls in areas where swimming crabs are abundant, especially the blue crab nursery grounds at the Sabine River offing[21] (East Texas), Caillou Bay, Terrebonne Parish (Louisiana) and Big Gulley, east of the Mobile Bay offing (Alabama). Crab nursery grounds occur in two types of marine habitat — shallow seagrass beds and the shallow mud bottom bays of coastal marshes. Other seabed types associated with ridley captures included sand, oyster shell and turtle grass (*Thalassia*).

XXXI Where You Can See Kemp's Ridleys:

(1) In Marine Aquariums

Head started turtles have been sent to marine aquariums (or oceanariums) in the United States and the British West Indies by the NMFS Galveston Laboratory. NMFS biologist Dickie Revera makes all arrangements for their trips and keeps an inventory of the captive stock, seeing to it that they are properly cared for by their keepers. These turtles act as a reserve stock for breeding the species in captivity.

Because of their easy living conditions, the turtles mature much earlier than their wild counterparts. Some of the eight-year-old head start turtles at the Cayman Turtle Farm in the British West Indies have produced several hundred hatchlings already. Two of these captive females laid their first eggs when only five years old, setting a record for the species. In the list that follows, the number of normal, head started Kemp's ridley turtles that could be viewed in the captive stock at marine aquariums in October, 1987, is shown in parenthesis. The total was then 103. The growth, behavior, environment and diet of these turtles are studied and evaluated during their captivity.

> Audubon Park and Zoological Gardens, New Orleans, LA (3)
> Bass Pro Shops, Springfield, MO (5)
> Cayman Turtle Farm, Grand Cayman, British West Indies (47)
> Clearwater Marine Science Center, Clearwater, FL (5)
> Dallas Aquarium, Dallas, TX (2)
> Marineland, Inc., St. Augustine, FL (8)
> Miami Seaquarium, Miami, FL (2)
> North Carolina Marine Resources Center, Kure Beach, NC (3)
> Pan American University, South Padre Island, TX (2)
> Sea-Arama Marineworld, Galveston, TX (18)
> Sea World of Florida, Orlando, FL (3)
> Theater of the Sea, Islamorado, FL (5)

Other head started turtles which cannot survive in the wild because of birth defects, injury or chronic illness are cared for and on educational display at:

> Sea Turtle Inc., South Padre Island, TX (3)
> Breckenridge Park Zoo, San Antonio, TX (3)
> Marine Life Park, Gulfport MS (1)

Sea Turtle Inc. and other marine aquariums also have wild Kemp's ridleys in captivity. These have been rehabilitated but are unable to survive in the wild, being permanently handicapped by serious injuries.

WHERE YOU CAN SEE KEMP'S RIDLEYS — (2) IN THE WILD

("Go shrimping" — Jack Woody.)

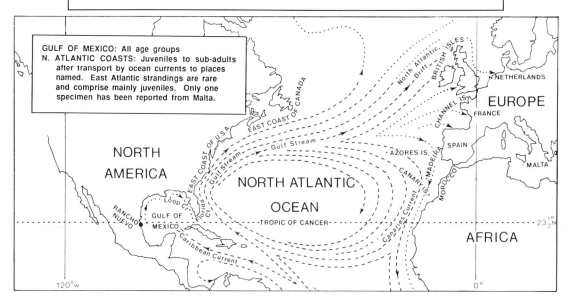

GULF OF MEXICO: All age groups
N. ATLANTIC COASTS: Juveniles to sub-adults after transport by ocean currents to places named. East Atlantic strandings are rare and comprise mainly juveniles. Only one specimen has been reported from Malta.

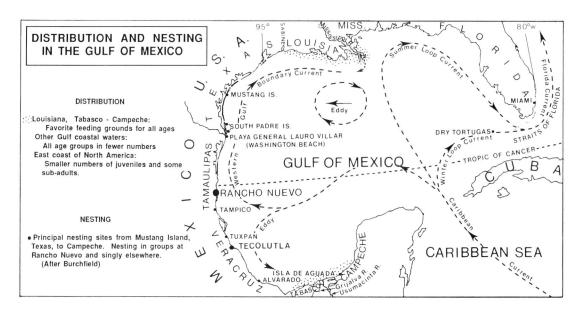

DISTRIBUTION AND NESTING IN THE GULF OF MEXICO

DISTRIBUTION

Louisiana, Tabasco - Campeche:
 Favorite feeding grounds for all ages
Other Gulf coastal waters:
 All age groups in fewer numbers
East coast of North America:
 Smaller numbers of juveniles and some sub-adults.

NESTING

• Principal nesting sites from Mustang Island, Texas, to Campeche. Nesting in groups at Rancho Nuevo and singly elsewhere.
 (After Burchfield)

XXXII A Cheerful Outlook?

THERE ARE GROUNDS FOR OPTIMISM about the future of the Kemp's ridley, quite apart from the fact that many highly capable and determined people are doing their level best to save the species. Larry Ogren, for one, is heartened by the large numbers of juvenile and sub-adult turtles that have appeared in the Gulf and along the Atlantic coast in recent years, presumably as a result of the conservation measures.

"Significant changes in the nature and distribution of the Kemp's ridley population have taken place in the last twenty years," says Ogren. "They have been caused by both the continued decline in numbers of adult turtles, and the strenuous efforts to protect their eggs.

"After the intensive egg harvesting of the fifties and early sixties reduced the size of a single arribada by over 92 per cent, by comparison with the nineteen-forties, sightings and captures of adult turtles became rare in the Gulf and very few hatchlings were produced at Rancho Nuevo. Neverthless the adult segment of the population was still much larger than it is today, particularly in relation to the number of juveniles and subadults.

"From the mid-sixties, after wholesale egg-taking was curtailed and the nesting turtles, eggs and hatchlings were protected from predators, there was still no protection for the adult and subadult turtles away from the nesting beach. The Mexican tagging program during this period demonstrated the vulnerability of the species to shrimp trawls. Gradually, over the last ten years, hatchlings produced by the conservation program at Rancho Nuevo (and head started yearlings from Galveston) have swelled the population in the Gulf, causing the present relative abundance of yearlings, juveniles and sub-adults."

With the new TED regulations in force, these turtles should live to take over from the few reproductively active adults that have survived. Compulsory use of TEDs by United States shrimp trawls should eliminate most of the mortalities that have been responsible for the annual 3 percent decline in the number of nesting ridleys during the eighties. There is a general hope that Mexico will introduce similar TED regulations.

It is because of the anticipated effects of the TEDs and the continued protection at Rancho Nuevo that Jack Woody, who a few years ago was recorded on videotape saying that he considered the Kemp's ridley as a species to be biologically extinct, now says: " ...I really expect to see a definite increase in the Kemp's nesting population within five to ten years, if not sooner."

"I am very optimistic about the results of the nest protection in Mexico and am an advocate of continuing and expanding this effort wherever the ridley nests," says Ogren. "All of this does suggest a slightly more optimistic future for the species. At least it encourages recovery efforts to be continued and expanded."

Mrs. Carole Allen, Chairperson of HEART, the thousands of school pupils and others who comprise its membership, and contributors, deserve special recognition for their practical and moral support of the head start research project, for increasing public awareness of the ridleys' plight and for promoting sea turtle conservation in general.

One third of the royalties from this book will go to HEART for Kemp's ridley sea turtle conservation.

"Working with these animals seems to inspire a remarkable concern that transcends scientific method. Perhaps the attitude of the beach workers reflects mankind's affection for turtles over all other reptiles. Turtles in general seem to demonstrate an enduring and persevering nature, qualities that humans profess to admire in themselves and others."

- Mrs. Miriam Korshak, Executive Producer, KUHT-TV Houston.

THE END

Acknowledgments

I AM MOST GRATEFUL to Dr. Charles W. Caillouet, Jr., Chief of the Life Studies Division of the National Marine Fisheries Service, Southeast Fisheries Center's Galveston Laboratory, who has generously devoted much time to informing, advising and encouraging us during the various stages of production of this book. My special thanks go also to Mrs Carole Allen, Chairperson of HEART, Houston, for her ideas, suggestions, insights and enthusiasm. It was a HEART open house at the Galveston Laboratory, organized by Mrs Allen, which first gave me the opportunity to become interested in Kemp's ridley sea turtles.

Professor Henry H. Hildebrand, from the former University of Corpus Christi, has been extremely helpful, as have Dr. René Márquez Millan, Chief of Turtle Conservation, Instituto Nacional de la Pesca, Mexico, and Mr. Jack B. Woody, National Sea Turtle Coordinator, United States Fish and Wildlife Service, Albuquerque, who supplied stories and information by telephone and fax and relayed messages from New Zealand to Dr. Márquez in Mexico. Dr. Peter C.H. Pritchard, Senior Vice-President of the Florida Audubon Society, gave invaluable advice, suggested the title of the book, and completely altered the direction of the book with his reminiscences about the early days at Rancho Nuevo. These appear almost exactly as he related them. Patrick M. Burchfield, General Curator-Herpetologist of the Gladys Porter Zoo, dictated many descriptions of life at Rancho Nuevo onto tapes and sent updates by fax.

Mr. Larry Ogren, Fishery Research Biologist at the NMFS Panama City Laboratory, supplied much valuable information, made helpful suggestions about the illustrations, and drove across Panama City many times to review maps, diagrams and additions to the script and discuss controversial issues by fax when time was short. Professor David Wm. Owens, of the Department of Biology, Texas A&M. University, College Station, also assisted generously.

Mr. and Mrs. Dearl Adams were a mine of information, sending scrapbook reports and photographs and answering interminable questions about their work in the sixties. Andrés Herrera Casasus obligingly supplied details of his discovery of the 1947 arribada and sent photocopies of his flight schedules from that time.

A great deal of assistance has also been received from other members of the staff of the NMFS at Galveston: Mrs Dickie B. Revera, who gave warm and caring encouragement and suggested a visit to Padre Island to see the imprinting, Mrs. Kathy Williams Indelicato, Mss. Sharon A. Manzella and Jo Ann Williams, Messrs. Clark T. Fontaine, Marcel J. Duronslet, William B. Jackson (who sent TED issue updates by fax) and Theodore D. Williams. I am also very grateful for help and advice from Mrs. Marjorie Carr; personnel of the National Park Service, Padre Island National Seashore, Corpus Christi, especially Mr. Bill Lukens, Mss. Jenny Bjork, Donna Shaver, Elizabeth Cheeseman, and Kirsten Brennan; Dr. Richard Byles, United States Fish and Wildlife Service, Albuquerque; Ms. Charlotte Delahay, Executive Assistant,and Mr. Michael Weber, Vice-President for Programs, Center for Environmental Education; Mrs. Miriam Korshak, Executive Producer, KUHT-TV, Houston, and producer of KUHT-TV's video *The Heart-break Turtle*; Mrs Ila Loetscher and Mrs. Evelyn Sizemore, Co-Directors of Sea Turtle Inc.; Mr. Douglas Beach, NMFS, Gloucester, Mass.; Ms. Barbara Schroeder, NMFS, Miami Laboratory, Miami, Florida; the Sea Turtle Stranding and Salvage Network, Miami, Florida; Messrs. Samuel S. Sadove (Research Director) and Stephen J. Morreale (Director of Sea Turtle Research) and Miss Rachel Yellin, Okeanos Ocean Research Foundation; Dr. Anne Barkau Meylan, Sea Turtle Coordinator, Bureau of Marine Research, State of Florida Department of Natural Resources; Mrs. Colleen Crow, designer of the HEART logo; and Dr. R.F.C. Claridge, Reader in Chemistry at the University of Canterbury, Christchurch, New Zealand, who helped with Spanish vocabulary.

I am also indebted for information from articles and scientific or technical papers by D.E. Adams, J.S. Bleakney, L.D. Brongersma, P.M. Burchfield, C.W. Caillouet, Jr., D.K. Caldwell, A.F. Carr, Center for Environmental Education, H. Chávez, K. Cliffton, M. Contreras G., B.A. Cox, R.W. Doughty, M.J. Duronslet, M.L. Edwards, L.M. Ehrhart, R.S. Felger, M. Fletcher, M.A. Grassman, G. Gunter, T.A. Henwood, T.P.E. Hernandez D., H.H. Hildebrand, M.C. Ingham, E.F. Klima, M. Lutcavage, C. McVea, Jr., J.P. McVey, R. Márquez M., N. Martin, R.G. Mauermann, A.B. Meylan, J.F. Mitchell, S.J. Morreale, N. Mrosovsky, S.R.H. Murphy, J.A. Mortimer, J.A. Musick, L.H. Ogren, D.W. Owens, P.C.H. Pritchard, R. Regal, D.B. Revera, S.S. Sadove, F.J.Schwartz, W.R. Seidel, A.K. Shah, J.R. Spotila, E.A. Standora, J.W. Watson, M. Weber, R.E. Willett, Jr. and C.L. Yntema also from technical reports from the NMFS (Galveston), the FWS (Endangered Species Office, Albuquerque), the NPS (PAIS), and from P.M. Burchfield et al. on the Republic of Mexico/United States of America conservation effort on behalf of the Kemp's ridley sea turtle at Playa de Rancho Nuevo, Tamaulipas, Mexico; and from books by Professor Archie Carr: *The Windward Road* (University Presses, Florida, 1956), *So Excellent a Fishe: A Natural History of Sea Turtles* (The Natural History Press, l967) and *Handbook of Turtles* (Cornell University Press, 1952); Jack Rudloe: *Time of the Turtle* (Knopf, 1979); Karen A. Bjorndal and George H. Balazs (editors): *Manual of Sea Turtle Research and Conservation Techniques*, Second Edition, (Center for Environmental Education, 1983); Francine Jacobs and Mary Beath (Illustrator): *Sea Turtles, A Coloring Book in English and Spanish* (Center for Environmental Education, 1981); and Yvette Metral and Charlotte Knox (Illustrator): *Animal World: The Turtle* (Rourke Enterprises, 1983). I wish to thank the following for allowing me to use quotations from books mentioned above: Mrs. Marjorie Carr (*So Excellent a Fishe*), Cornell University Press (*Handbook of Turtles*) and Jack Rudloe (*Time of the Turtle*).

The illustrations are based on photographs taken by Dr. Caillouet, Daniel Patlan and other participants in the Operation Head Start Project, especially Dr. Pritchard, Pat Burchfield, Sharon Manzella and Dr. Byles; by Dearl Adams,

Andrés Herrera, Dr. Meylan, Bill Pogue (in Robert E. Willett, Jr.'s *Solving the Riddle of the Ridley* in *Exxon U.S.A.*, first quarter 1986, Vol XXV No 1), Norman Martin (in his article *Mission Possible*, in *Texas Shores*, Summer 1986), C. Allan Morgan, Carlos Hernandez, and myself. The illustrations on the front and back covers are based on photographs taken by Bill Pogue and Sharon Manzella, respectively. I am grateful to the Rijksmuseum van Natuurlijke Historie, Leiden, the Netherlands, for granting permission to use Plate 10 from an article on European Atlantic turtles by L.D. Brongersma, in *Zoologische Verhandelingen* Nr. 121.

Drs. Caillouet and Pritchard, Professor Hildebrand and Mrs. Allen most kindly reviewed the manuscript at several stages. I am grateful to Mrs Carr, Dr. Márquez, Jack Woody, Professor Owens, Larry Ogren, Pat Burchfield, Dr. Byles, Jenny Bjork, Donna Shaver, and Dearl Adams for also reviewing the whole manuscript, and to the following for reviewing sections of it: Mrs. Revera, Dr. Meylan, Mrs. Sizemore, Mrs. Indelicato, Mss. Schroeder, Manzella, and Williams, Dr. McVey and Messrs. Beach, Duronslet, Fontaine, Sadove and Morreale. Janie Lowe, Lisa Ulvick, Mrs. Chris Dunning and Sarah (aged 11) and Mark (aged 9) Dunning, and our sons John and Timothy, also read the manuscript and made helpful comments.

I also wish to acknowledge the kindness of our friends Wilf and Mil Jonah, who sailed my husband Leon and me to the various bays and reefs in the British and United States Virgin Islands where the Director of the British Virgin Islands National Parks Trust, Dr. Nicholas Clarke, had advised that we would be able to snorkel among green and hawksbill turtles.

Finally I wish to thank Leon for his encouragement, advice, assistance and cooperation, which extended to imprinting hatchlings for three days at Padre Island and hoisting Jimmy Junior from Ila Loetscher's tank for a photograph.

Footnotes

[1] Specimen used to establish and characterize a new species or subspecies of animal or plant.

[2] Jack Rudloe, Time of the Turtle (Knopf, l979).

[3] Larry Ogren writes concerning the Kemp's ridley: "The small orbit located high on the skull above the deep upper jaw creates a parrot-like appearance — thus the Spanish vernacular name for this species, Tortuga Lora." (Lora and cotorra both mean parro$_t$).

[4] Currently Director of the Houston Zoo.

[5] Biologists studying fish (ichthyologists) or amphibians and reptiles (herpetologists).

[6] Arribada: Spanish for arrival, pronounced ahr-ree-BAH-dah. Used to describe the simultaneous appearance of many turtles on the nesting beach or in the water nearby.

[7] Dearl E. Adams, in International Turtle & Tortoise Society Journal, Volume 1, September - October, 1966.

[8] Publication No. 17, Instituto Nacional de Investigaciones Biologico Pesqueras; International Turtle and Tortoise Society Journal, Volume 2, Nos. 4 & 5, 1968.

[9] Here we follow the Spanish custom of writing the mother's surname last. This is the same person as the René Márquez mentioned earlier.

[10] P.C.H. Pritchard and René Márquez M., Monograph No. 2, Marine Turtle Series. International Union for Conservation of Nature and Natural Resources, Morges, Switzerland, 1973.

[11] P.C.H. Pritchard, Report on United States/Mexico Conservation of Kemp's Ridley Sea Turtle at Rancho Nuevo, Tamaulipas, Mexico, in 1979. U.S. Fish and Wildlife Service.

[12] Fishery guide or instructions; a Pesca document.

[13] For the sake of accuracy we have to admit that turtle eggs do not become hard when boiled. For this reason cakes stay fresh and moist longer when baked with turtle eggs.

[14] Experimenters in biology use the term control for a comparison experiment in which the effect studied should be absent.

[15] Sea Turtles, a coloring book in English and Spanish, Francine Jacobs and Mary Beath (Illustrator), Center for Environmental Education, Washington D.C., 1981.

[16] It would be insensitive to make the comparison with a soup plate.

[17] Anne Barkau Meylan, in Natural History, volume 11, page 90 (1986).

[18] "About thirty days later is our best guess," David Owens says.

[19] NOAA Technical Memorandum NMFS-SEFC-201, January 1988, Annual Report of the Galveston Laboratory for fiscal year1987.

[20] A striking poster: Sea Turtles of the World, designed by Peter Pritchard and painted by M. Bennett, Jr., is available from the Center for Environmental Education.

[21] Offing: position offshore from the named location.

Index of Illustrations

Index